AF386497

# J. M. W. TURNER
## The 'Skies' Sketchbook

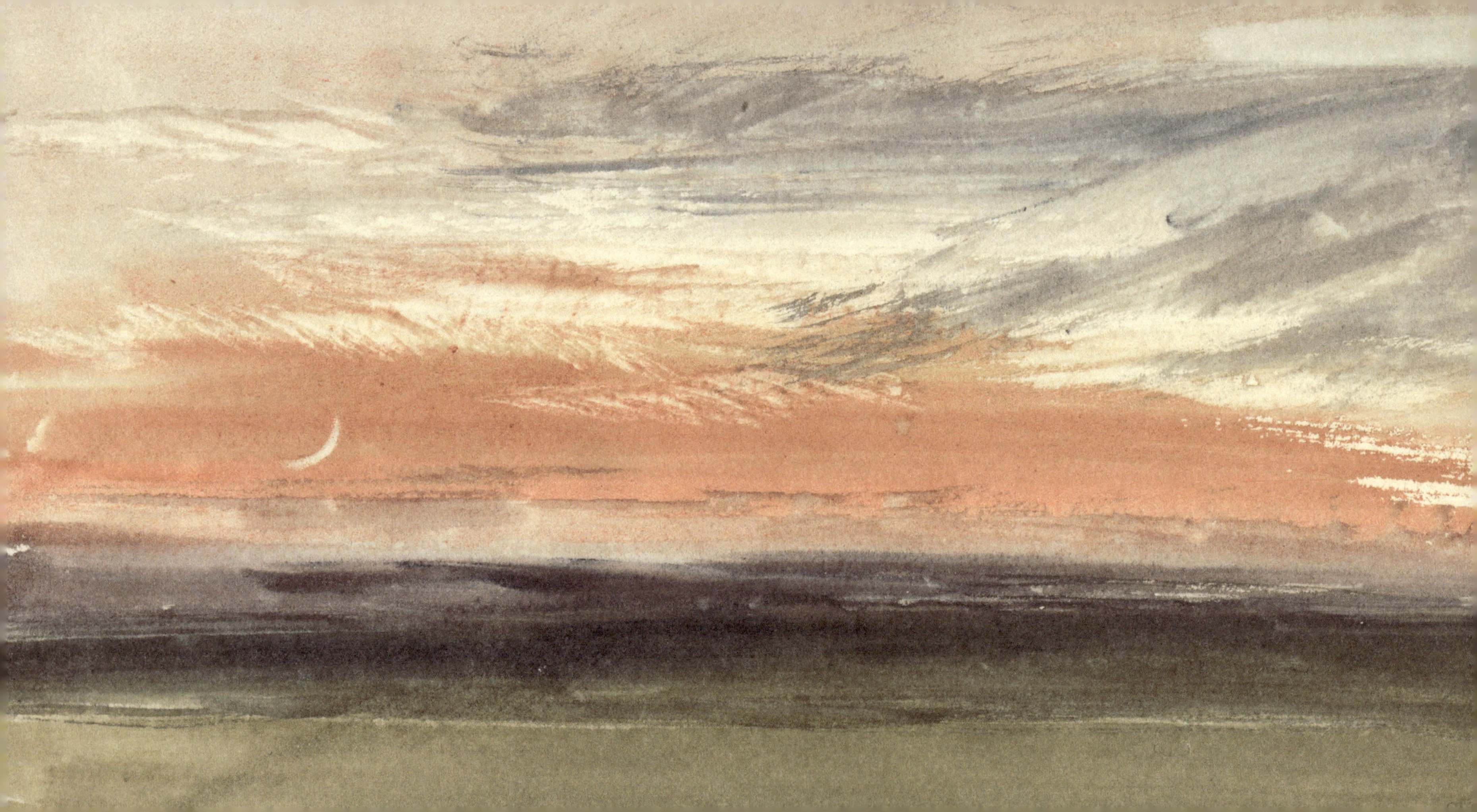

# J. M. W. TURNER

## The 'Skies' Sketchbook

With an introduction by
David Blayney Brown

TATE PUBLISHING

First published 2016 by order of the Tate Trustees
by Tate Publishing, a division of Tate Enterprises Ltd,
Millbank, London SW1P 4RG
www.tate.org.uk/publishing

Reprinted 2017, 2019, 2021, 2024



A catalogue record for this book is available from the British Library

ISBN 978 1 84976 490 2

Distributed in the United States and Canada by ABRAMS, New York
Library of Congress Control Number: applied for

Designed by Libanus Press Ltd
Colour reproduction by DL Imaging, London
Printed by Tecnostampa, Pigini Group – Printing Division, Italy

Front cover: J.M.W. Turner, *The 'Skies' Sketchbook* c.1817, folio 4
Frontispiece: J.M.W. Turner, *The 'Skies' Sketchbook* c.1817 (detail), folio 54

Measurements of artworks are given in centimetres, height before width
All sketchbook pages c.12.5 × 24.7

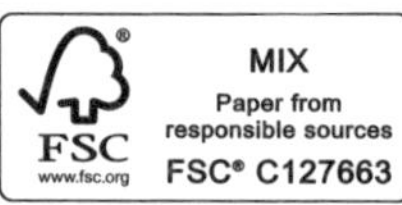

# INTRODUCTION

*David Blayney Brown*

Turner's sketchbooks were private things that he kept to himself. They might live for some time in his coat pockets or travel bags, to be pulled out as the need arose. In the studio, they served as memory banks for future work. This does not necessarily mean that he used them haphazardly, but that their contents and outcomes can span years or seem disparate at first glance. Besides many watercolour studies of sky effects, the sketchbook reproduced here includes pencil sketches, apparently entered from the opposite end (the back as the pages are now numbered), of places in London and nearby associated with Turner's friend and patron Walter Fawkes. Several of these are datable to 1818 or later but the sketchbook could have been used earlier as its pages, made by J. Whatman, are dated 1814 in the watermark. Organising his sketchbooks years later, Turner labelled it '79. Skies', positioning it immediately after one used in 1816 while visiting Fawkes at his Yorkshire seat, Farnley Hall.

Turner drew and painted the sky, clouds and weather all his life. As a boy he liked to go up to Hampstead Heath, lie on his back to draw the sky, and return to town to sell his day's work. Late in life he made many coloured studies, often in Kent – he believed the Isle of Thanet had the finest skies in Europe. In notes made about 1810 for his lectures as Professor of Perspective at the Royal Academy, he praised 'our variable climate, where the seasons are recognizable in one day . . . vapoury turbulence involves the face of things [and] nature seems to sport in all her dignity'.[1] He planned to tell his audience of young artists that 'endless variety is on our side and opens a new field of novelty'. He was far from unique in the practice of what his fellow painter John Constable called 'skying'. For many artists it was part of a new quest for naturalism, an attempt to bring empirical or would-be scientific observation to bear on natural phenomena, as Luke Howard did in his pioneering book *The Climate of London* published from 1818.[2] But for the Romantic imagination the sky was also a window into heaven, a glimpse of the divine or a space where earthly dramas were foretold or repeated. Constable declared that a painter 'who does not make his skies a very material part of his composition – neglects to avail himself of one of his greatest aids' and his 'chief organ of sentiment'.[3] Turner could never be accused of such neglect. Even so, the sustained concentration on the sky demonstrated in this sketchbook is exceptional, surely reflecting extraordinary weather conditions at the time.

On 10 April 1815, Mount Tambora at Sumbawa in the Dutch East Indies (now Indonesia) erupted in the most spectacular and devastating volcanic explosion in recorded history, throwing a plume of dust and gas into the atmosphere. For almost three years, skies around the world went dark or developed a baleful, infernal glow as the sun or moon struggled to break through. Crops failed; famine, cholera and typhus ran rampant, killing millions; riots and insurrection broke out in many countries, threatening anarchy, terrifying governments and creating an apocalyptic, millenarian mood to match the prevailing gloom. Wounded veterans of the Napoleonic Wars that ended at Waterloo in June 1815, two months after the eruption, were joined by starving beggars on the streets of Europe's cities. 1816 turned into a 'year without a summer'. By Lake Geneva that July, Byron began his poem 'Darkness' with the words 'I had a dream, which was not all a dream. The bright sun was extinguish'd ...' His guest Mary Shelley, housebound by 'perpetual rain', started work on her nightmare novel *Frankenstein* (1818). While writers indulged their imaginations with the supernatural, Turner had to battle the weather to fulfil a commission for 120 views of Richmondshire. He spent the summer in Yorkshire, reporting from Farnley in September: 'Rain, rain, rain, day after day. Italy deluged, Switzerland a wash-pot ... Lakes all in *one*'.[4] News of the dire conditions on the Continent probably came from his host Fawkes, whose friend the Earl of Darlington had been travelling in the Rhineland. Even without a task that Turner could combine with a long visit to Fawkes – anyway now an annual fixture – it was not an auspicious time to venture abroad. His own tour of the Rhine and battlefield of Waterloo in 1817 may have been postponed from the previous year.

Dreadful weather everywhere, confinement to England, deferred European travel and the friendship and patronage of Fawkes and his circle all underpin the images in this sketchbook. Rendered in a variety of watercolour techniques, wet and dry, transparent and solid, the skies seem to fall into categories: damp, cloudy and breezy, typically English (folios 3, 4, 19); others more sombre or stormy with a heavy reddish tint; daylight, twilight and night-time (folios 45, 54). A pencil sketch inside the back cover has colour notes, recording direct observation. Elsewhere, as with all coloured sky studies where an artist must struggle to keep up with constantly changing effects, the question arises how true they are, seen outdoors or through a window, or how far remembered or invented, perhaps in this case to re-imagine or escape from the grim realities of 1815 and 1816. They are hard to date or place exactly, lacking any features save for a hint of a horizon or silhouette of trees (folio 41). Although overcast skies are present throughout the series of Rhine watercolours that Turner made in 1817, giving them what his first biographer called a 'subdued and regretful air',[5] where indicated at all in the sketchbook land is mostly flat or gently undulating, leading to suggestions that it was used in the Low Countries en route. If so it could also have been employed in the north of England immediately afterwards, as Turner still had the sketchbooks from the tour with him when he visited Lord Darlington and Fawkes in late summer. It has also been proposed that a few of the warmer-toned skies are Italian, dating from Turner's visit to Rome and Naples in 1819; there are glimpses of stone pines, and similarities to coloured studies Turner made in Italy (folios 42, 52). In the absence of other topographical markers, perhaps the most that can be said is that while the extended weather shock beginning in 1815 focused Turner's interest on the sky, the studies in this sketchbook show – in varying degrees – the recovery from it; the moon shines clear again, clouds thin, the artist can venture out, sketchbook in hand.

Another way to look at this sketchbook is through watercolours and pictures painted in the same few years, 1816–19. These too have exceptionally vivid or significant skies and it would be surprising if Turner did not refer to the sketchbook while mapping them out. As well as the Rhine watercolours, finished by Turner at Lord Darlington's seat, Raby Castle, shortly after returning to England, and sold to Fawkes as soon as he reached Farnley, Richmondshire watercolours like *Lancaster Sands*

– which Fawkes also acquired – include spectacular skies (pl.1). Oil paintings are still more dramatic. While at Raby, Turner began work for Lord Darlington on a view of the castle, its parkland and celebrated hunt (pl.2). Seen from rising ground the castle lies in a dip in the rolling landscape, sunlight and showers contending overhead. If such a battle of weathers sounds far-fetched, it is worth remembering that one of Darlington's hounds, drawn and identified by Turner in another sketchbook from

PL.1. *Lancaster Sands* c.1818, watercolour on paper 28 × 36.6. Birmingham Museum and Art Gallery, Birmingham

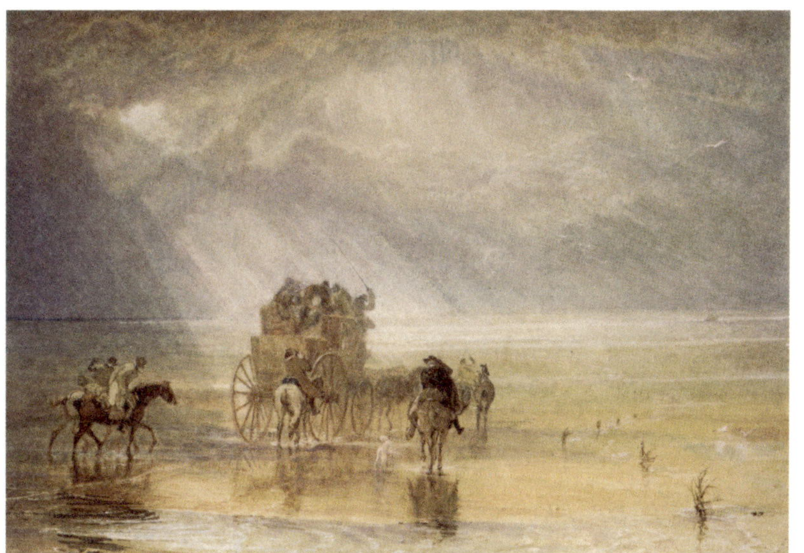

PL.2. *Raby Castle, The Seat of the Earl of Darlington* 1818, oil paint on canvas 119 × 180.6. The Walters Art Gallery, Baltimore, Maryland

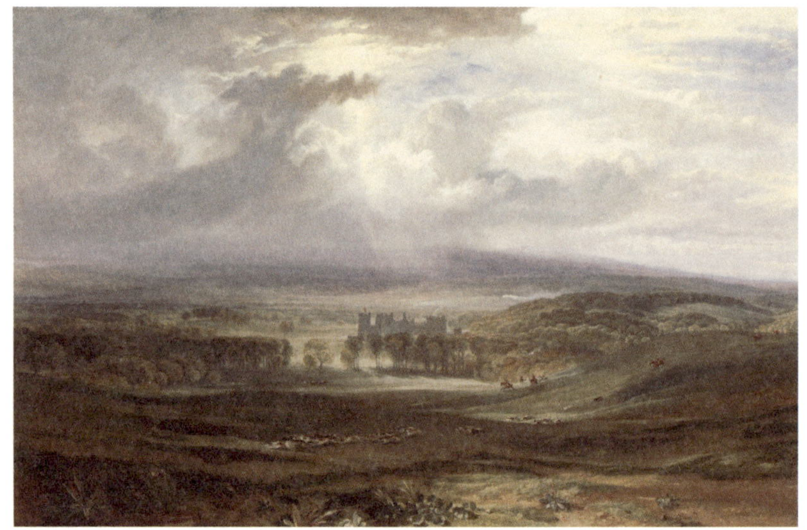

1817, was called Blücher after the commander of the Prussian troops fighting alongside the British at Waterloo. And Turner has matched the hunt careering across the estate, Blücher presumably at the forefront, with a sky where 'nature sports in all her dignity' just as he had once described.

Not surprisingly, the most magnificently gloomy sky that Turner painted in this period hangs over *The Field of Waterloo* (pl.3), one of three pictures based on the

1817 tour. This is a night sky, lit up like the post-battle carnage by slivers of moonlight behind cloud, an exploding flare and the fire still burning in the farm at Hougoumont where some of the bloodiest fighting took place. Here the darkness evokes the horror of war but probably draws on memories of volcanic winter too. Turner exhibited the picture with an epigraph from Byron's *Childe Harold's Pilgrimage* (1812–18) describing the menacing thunderclouds that closed over the battlefield 'which when rent/the earth is covered thick with other clay'. A watercolour of the subject painted around the same time for Fawkes has a similarly emotive sky, as do later illustrations made for

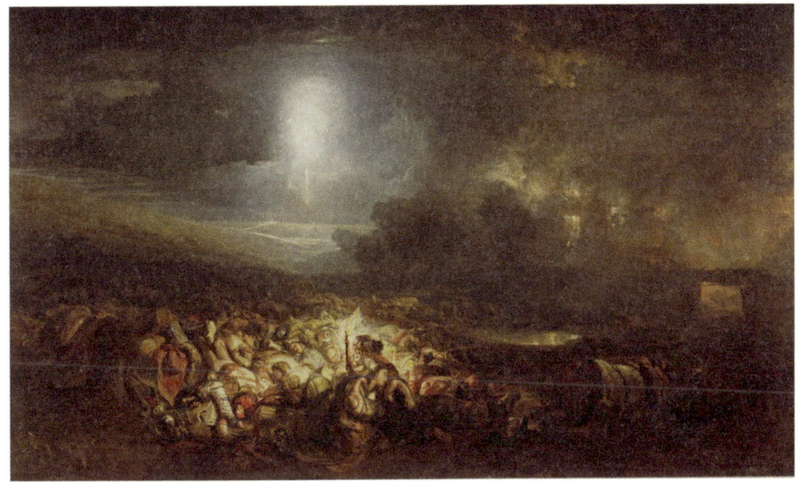

Byron and Walter Scott, where it mirrors the conflict below; in the Scott illustration, a bolt of lightning strikes the spot where General Picton was killed. With *Waterloo* in 1818, Turner exhibited a contrastingly tranquil Dutch canal scene, *Dort or Dordrecht: the Dort Packet-Boat from Rotterdam Becalmed* (pl.4); together, they symbolise war and peace. In *Dort*, trade and travellers have returned to the Dutch waterways, if temporarily held up by lack of wind. With the weather back to its normal patterns the

PL.4. *Dort or Dordrecht: the Dort Packet-Boat from Rotterdam Becalmed* 1818, oil paint on canvas 157.5 × 233.7. Yale Center for British Art, Paul Mellon Collection, New Haven, Connecticut

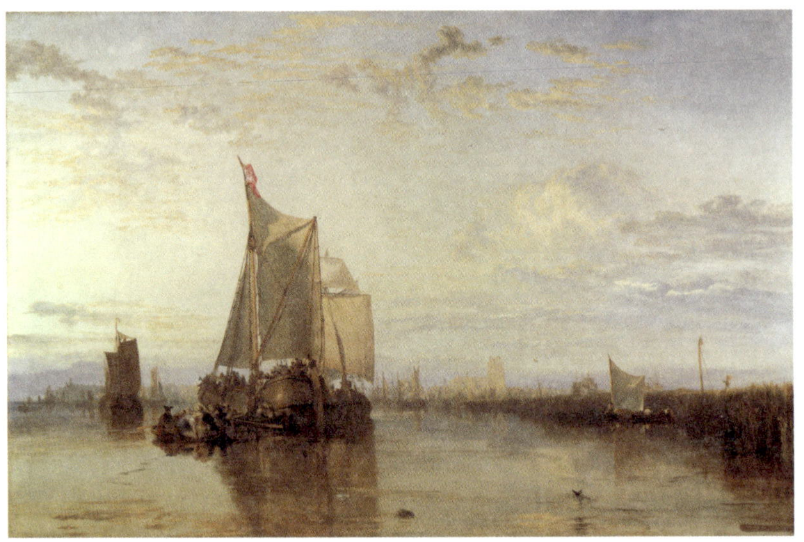

vast sky is clear and sunlit, flecked with strands of pearly cloud like those painted two centuries earlier by the Dordrecht painter Aelbert Cuyp. Perhaps the most remarkable sky from this period is to be seen in *Entrance of the Meuse: Orange-Merchant on the Bar, Going to Pieces* ...(pl.5) exhibited in 1819. It too is Cuypish, but breezier and unstable, to fit events below: the wreck of a cargo of oranges on a treacherous sand-bank – a visual pun for the financial crash facing the former Prince of Orange, King

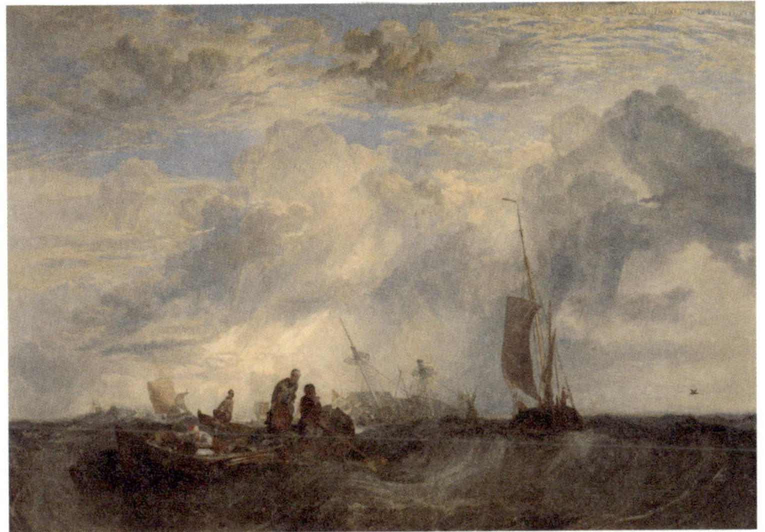

PL.5. *Entrance of the Meuse: Orange-Merchant on the Bar, Going to Pieces; Brill Church Bearing S.E by S., Masensluys E. by S.* 1819, oil paint on canvas 175.3 × 246.4. Tate. Accepted by the nation as part of the Turner Bequest 1856

William I of the United Netherlands after his wartime investments in Britain turned sour. This sketchbook could have provided inspiration for the dynamic cloudscape (folios 3, 4, 19).

Neither *Waterloo* nor *Entrance of the Meuse* sold, remaining on Turner's hands, but *Dort* was bought by Fawkes – as the greatest of his many works by Turner – and installed at Farnley. In April 1819, at his London house, 45 Grosvenor Place, Fawkes honoured Turner with an exhibition of the finest watercolours he had bought from him during their years of friendship. Turner himself recorded the hang in the East Drawing Room, with many works recognisable today, as well as the décor of this handsome Regency interior (pl.6). It is not quite the same as drawn in this sketchbook (folio 69a), where swagged fabric is gathered in rosettes below the cornice. Could this be a rejected idea for protecting the walls during the exhibition? Nearby in the sketchbook Turner drew the exterior of the house (folio 66a), and a double-page spread of the view from its windows across the grounds of Buckingham House (shown before its redesign by John Nash in 1825) to Westminster Abbey, the City and St Paul's (folios 68, 67a), which he used as the basis of a watercolour for Fawkes (pl.7) who had attended Westminster School (hidden by trees in the sketch). Turner was a regular guest at Grosvenor Place as well as at Farnley, adopted into the Fawkes family and taken on their outings. Sketches of the Fourth of June at Eton (folios 64a–66) and the nearby village of Salt Hill (folio 61a) must date from 1818, when Mrs Fawkes wrote in her diary for 4 June: 'Went to Eton to see the boat race. Dined and slept at Salt Hill. Little Turner came with us'.[6] Perhaps the party stayed at the Windmill Inn, sometimes

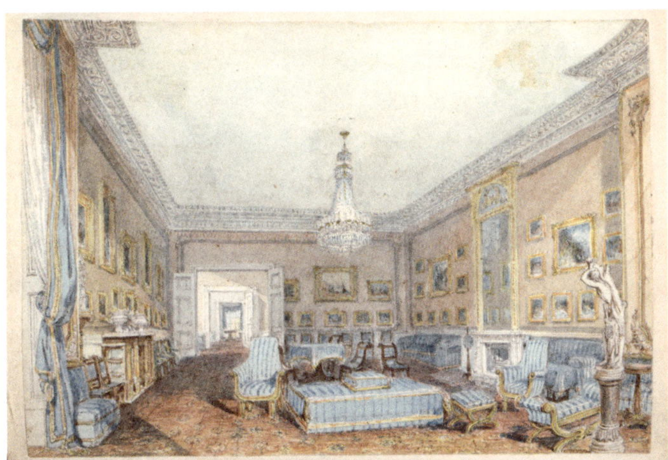

PL.6. *The East Drawing Room, 45 Grosvenor Place* 1819, watercolour on paper 15.2 × 21.6. Private collection

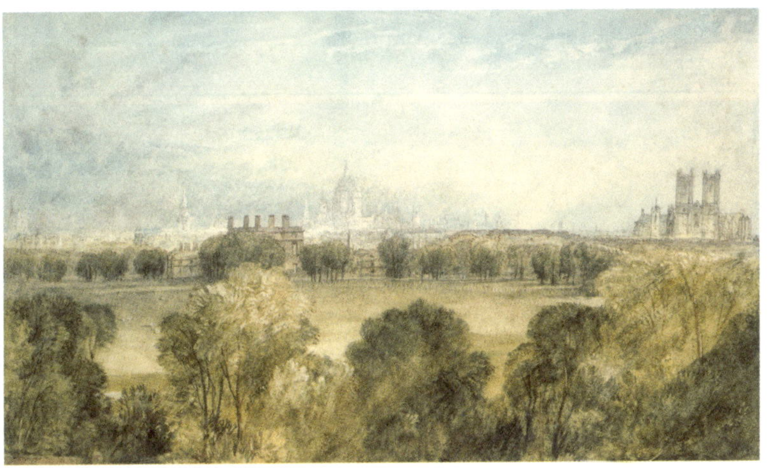

PL.7. *London, from the Windows of 45 Grosvenor Place* c.1819, watercolour on paper 25 × 39. Private collection

known as Botham's Hotel, the more fashionable of the village's two coaching inns, where in 1814 the Prince Regent had hosted a breakfast for the allied rulers, the King of Prussia, Emperor of Russia and the aforementioned Prince of Orange, and the Shelleys stayed the following year. Despite good views of Windsor, the Castle Inn may have been less inviting, having famously poisoned some guests with its turtle soup.

It will now be clear why Turner placed this sketchbook after one used at Farnley and in Yorkshire in 1816 while naming it 'Skies'. It reflects friendships, interests and activities while being pervaded by the impact and memory of the crisis in the world's weather beginning in the East Indies in 1815 and reaching Europe the following year. One subject remains to be mentioned, relating to Turner's long-standing series of landscape prints: the *Liber Studiorum*. The expedition with Mr and Mrs Fawkes and a

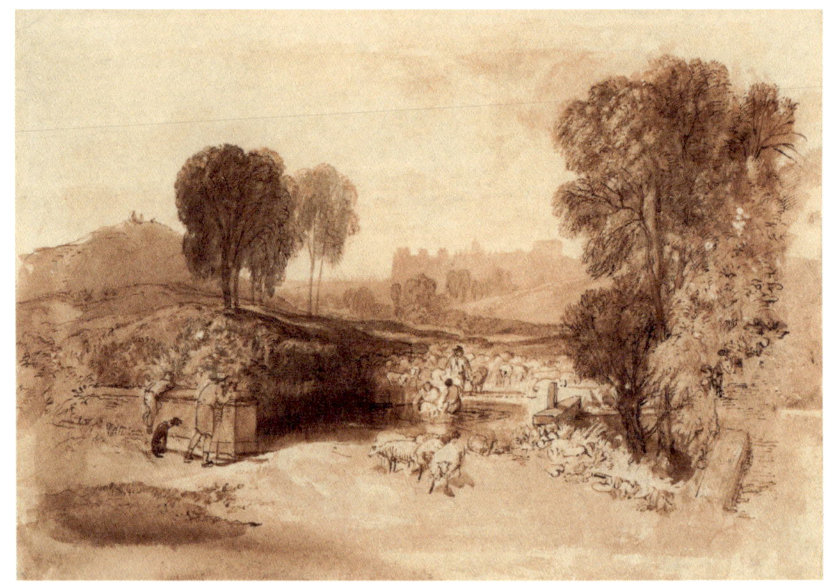

PL.8. *Windsor Castle from Salt Hill* ('*Sheep-washing, Windsor*') c.1818, watercolour on paper 22.7 × 31.6. Tate. Bequeathed by Henry Vaughan 1900

sketch of sheep-dipping in the river with Windsor Castle in the distance (folio 62a) inspired a new design, which Turner called 'Salt Hill' or 'Sheep-washing'. It was never published but the preparatory drawing (pl.8), and a proof plate etched by Turner himself and engraved by Charles Turner, reveals a luminous English pastoral, untouched by recent trauma.

NOTES

1 Lecture notes in John Gage, *Colour in Turner: Poetry and Truth*, London 1969, p.213.
2 Luke Howard, *The Climate of London: Deduced from Meteorological Observations Made in Different Places in the Neighbourhood of the Metropolis*, London 1818 (vol.I), 1820 (vol.II) and 1833 (revised edn with vol.III).
3 R.B. Beckett (ed.), *John Constable's Correspondence*, vol.6, Ipswich 1968, p.76.
4 John Gage (ed.), *Collected Correspondence of J.M.W. Turner with an Early Diary and Memoir by George Jones*, Oxford 1980, p.70.
5 Walter Thornbury, *The Life of J.M.W. Turner R.A., Founded on Letters and Papers Furnished by his Friends and Fellow Academicians*, London 1877, p.87.
6 A.J. Finberg, *A Complete Inventory of the Drawings of the Turner Bequest*, vol.I, London 1909, p.453.

FURTHER READING

Luke Herrmann, 'Skies, drawings of', in Evelyn Joll, Martin Butlin and Luke Herrmann (eds.), *The Oxford Companion to J.M.W. Turner*, Oxford 2001, pp.301–2.
Eric Shanes, *J.M.W. Turner. A Life in Art. Young Mr Turner: The First Forty Years 1775–1815*, New Haven and London 2016.
Ian Warrell, *Turner's Sketchbooks*, London 2014, pp.100–3.
Andrew Wilton, *The Life and Work of J.M.W. Turner*, Freiburg 1979.

No. 159 CLVIII CLVIII
Geo Jones

C. L. E.

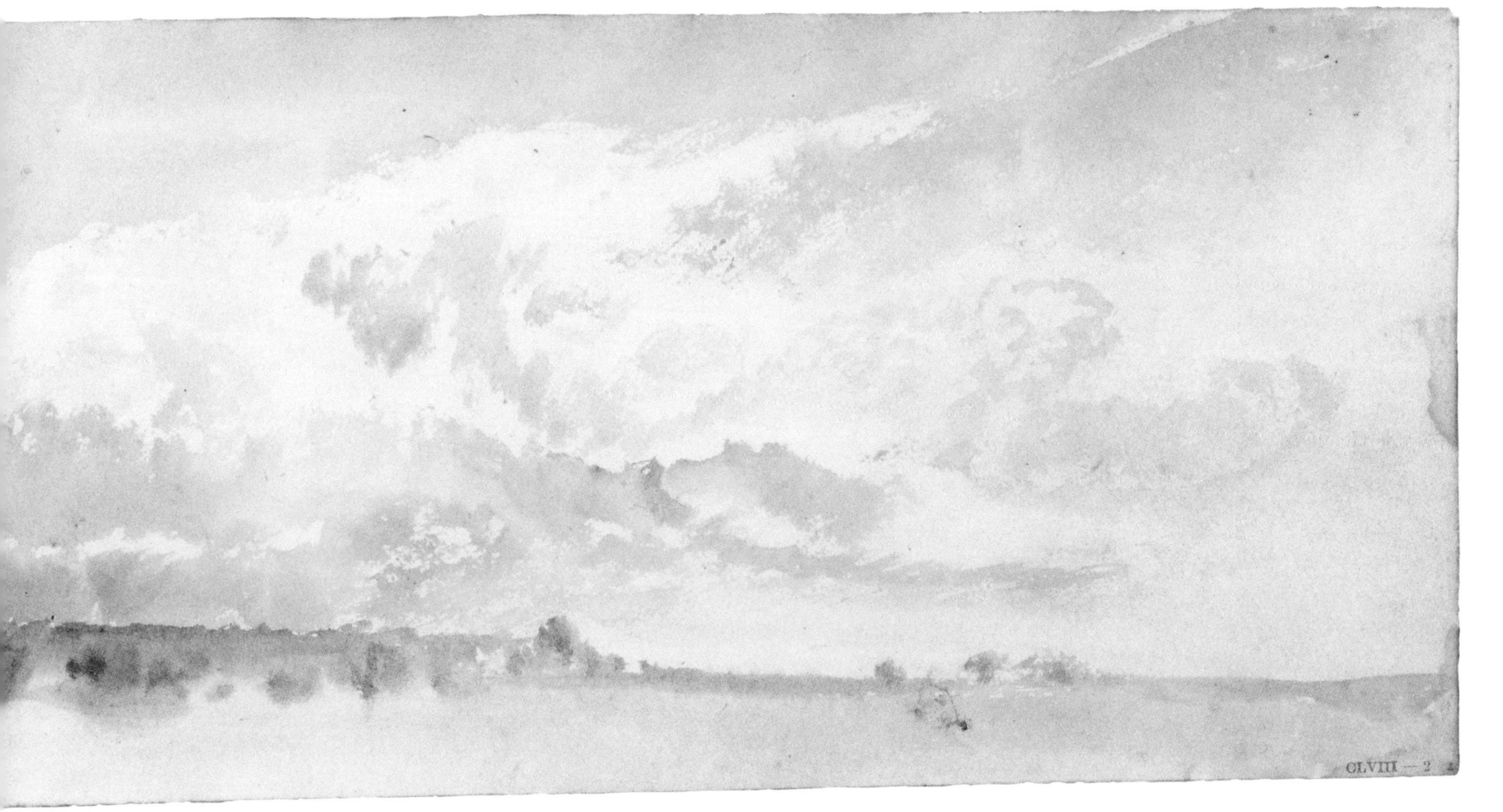
CLVIII — 2

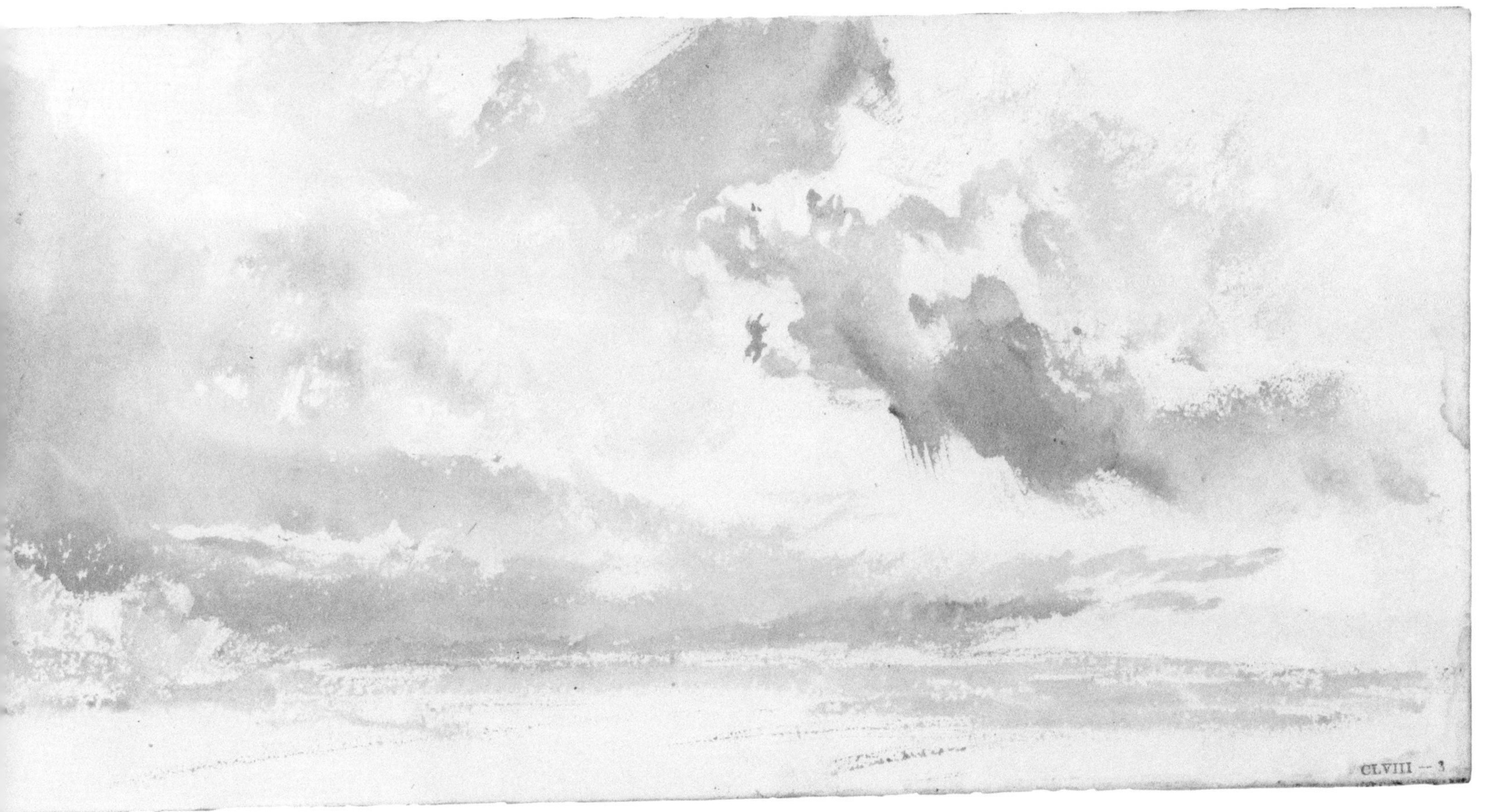

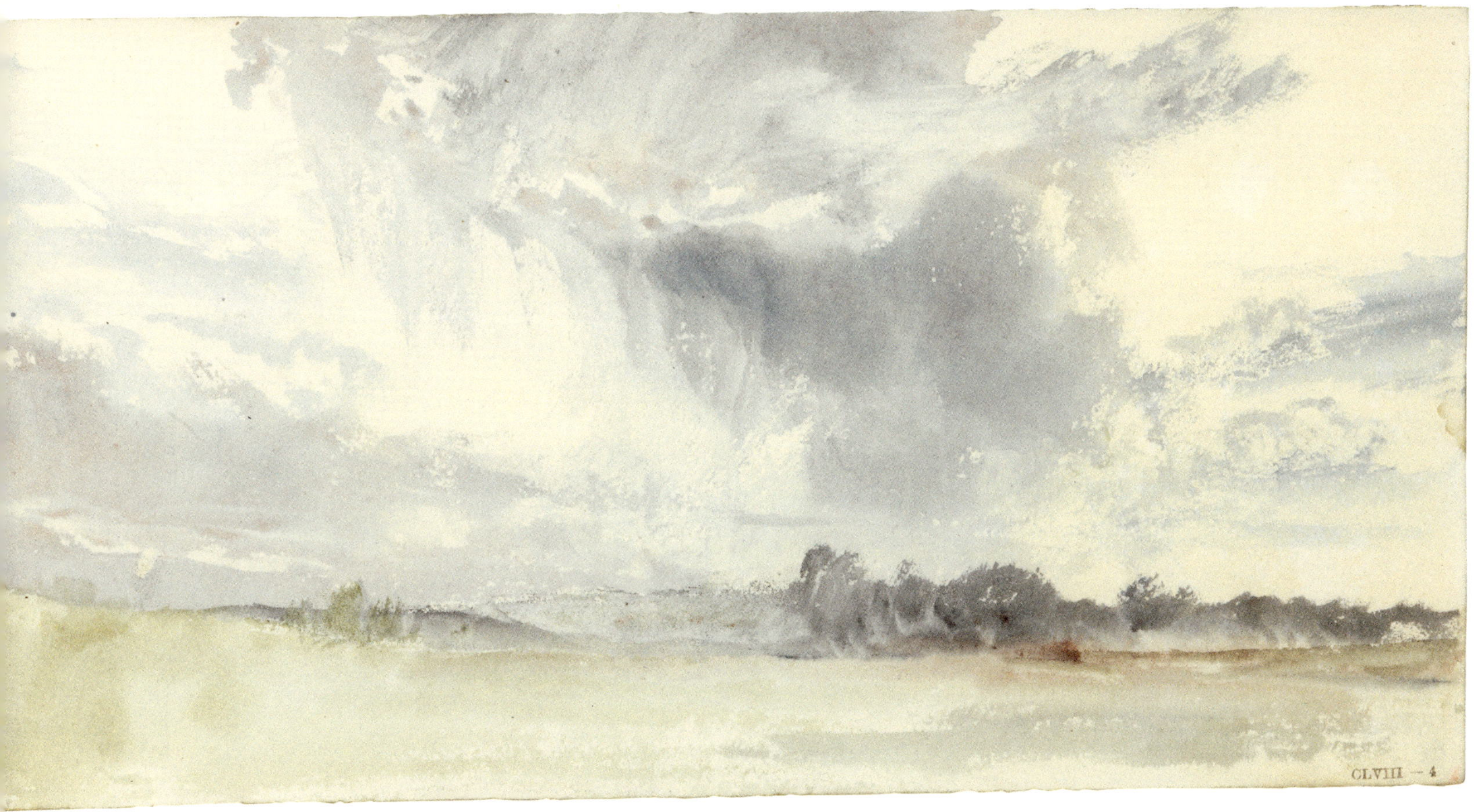
CLVIII — 4

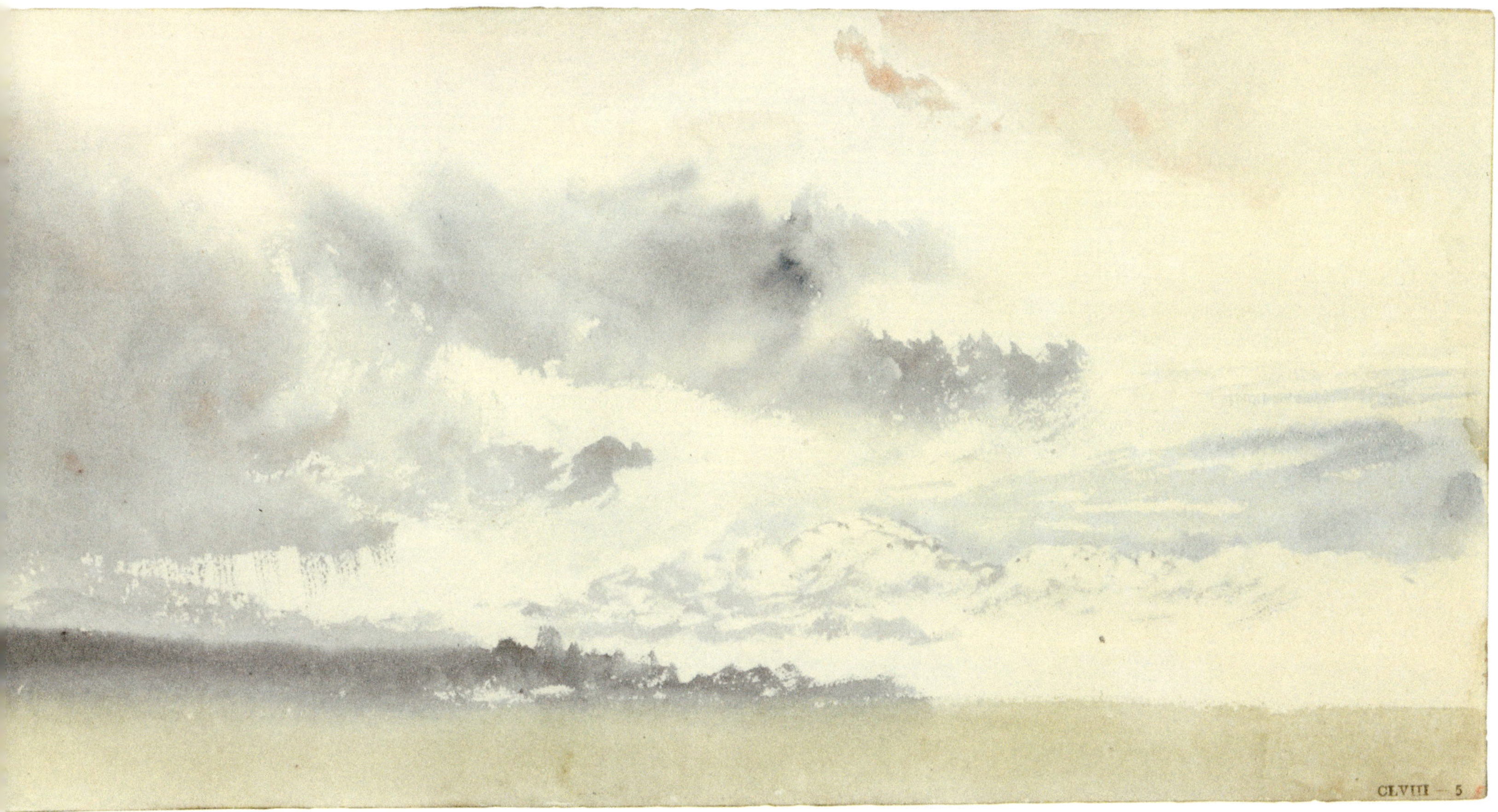
CLVIII — 5

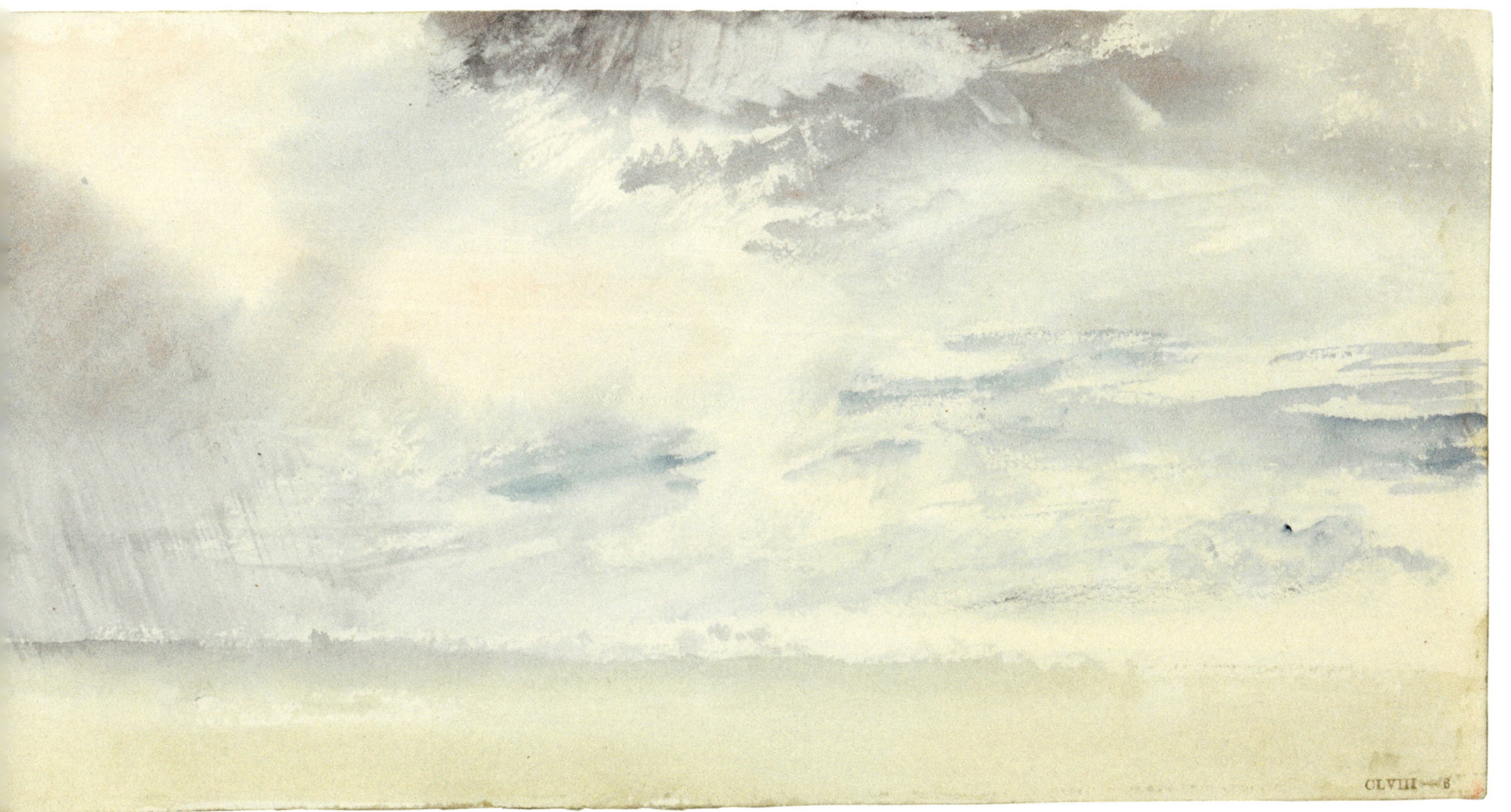
CLVIII — 6

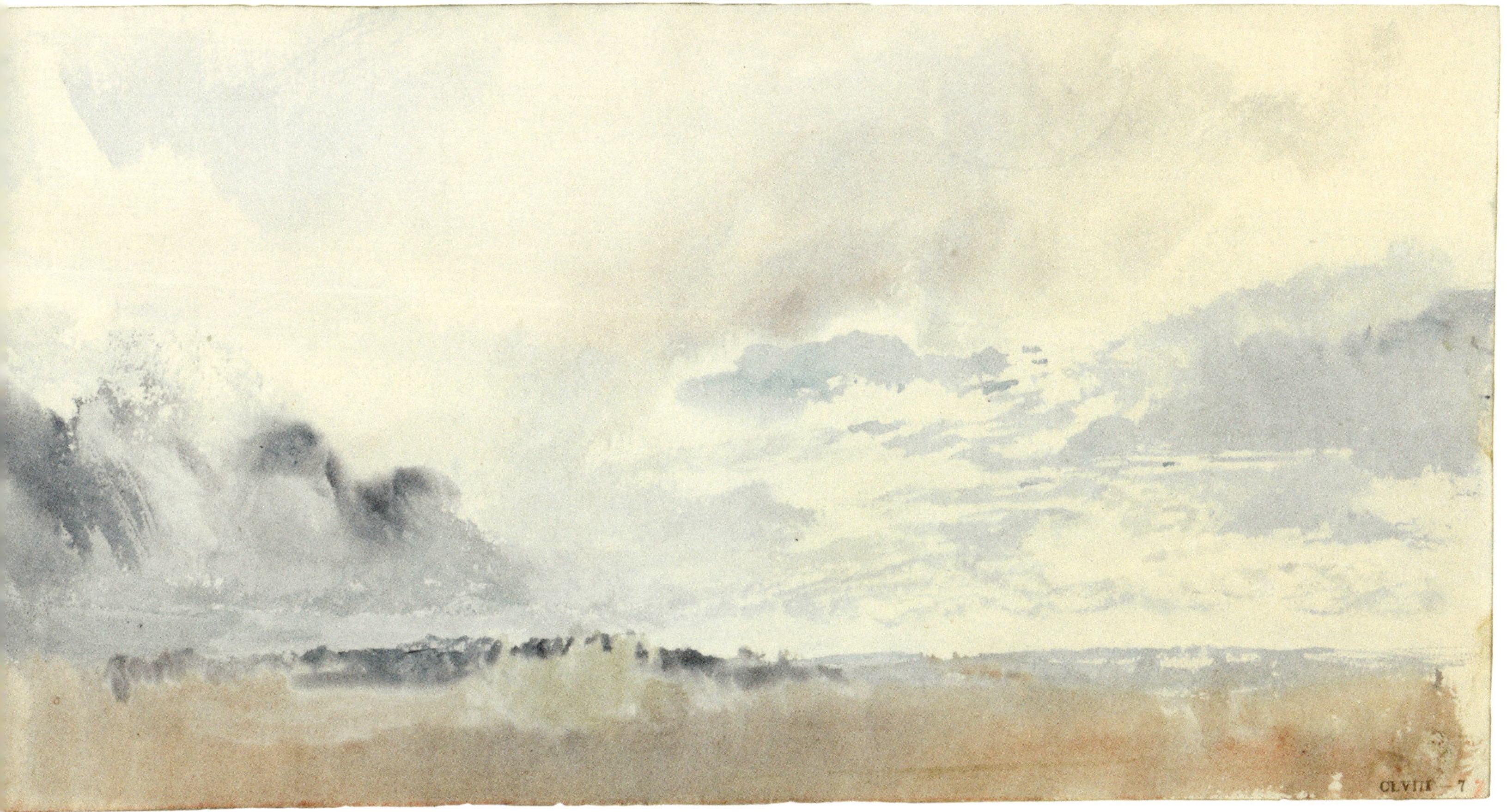
CLVIII — 7

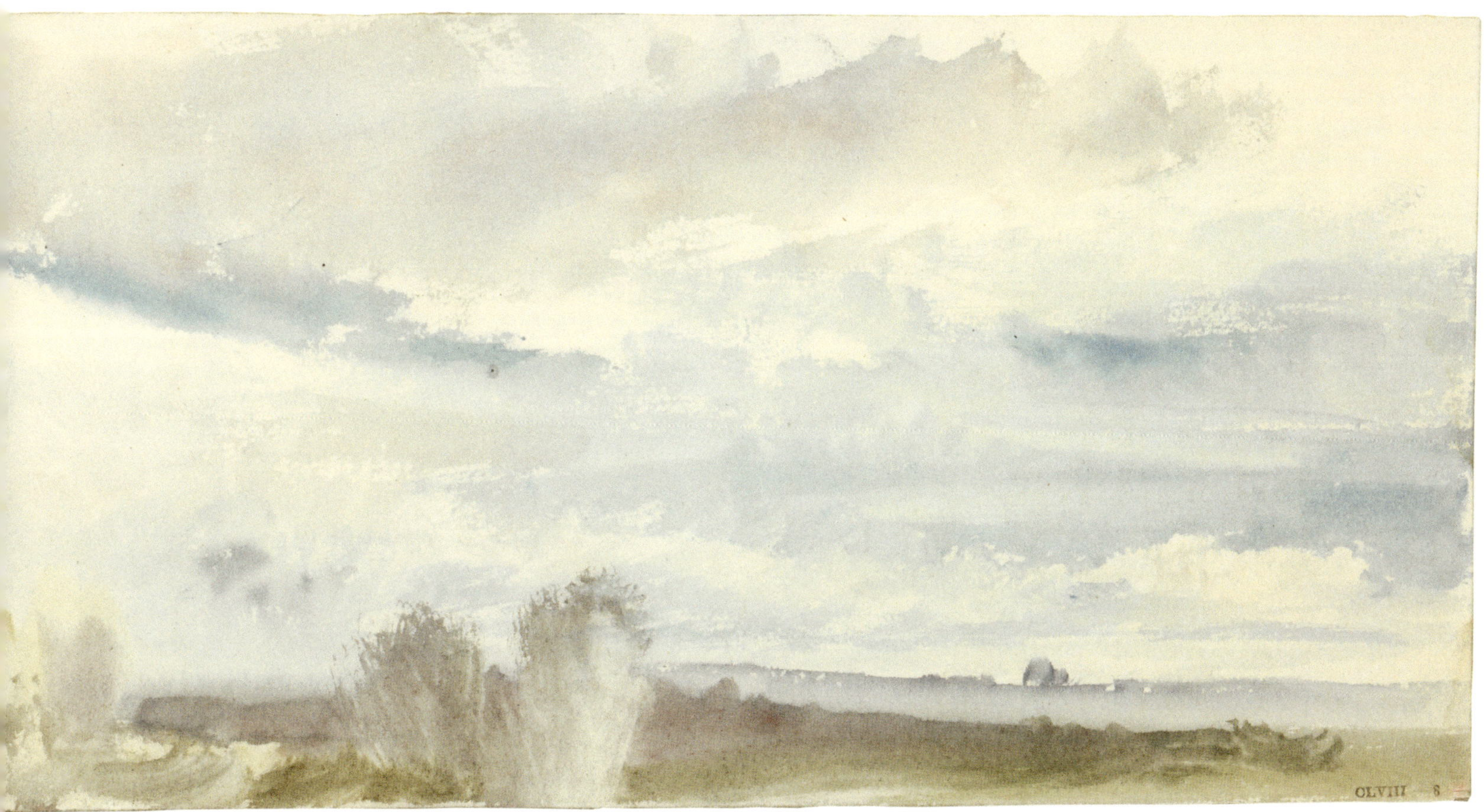
CLVIII – 8

CLVIII — 9

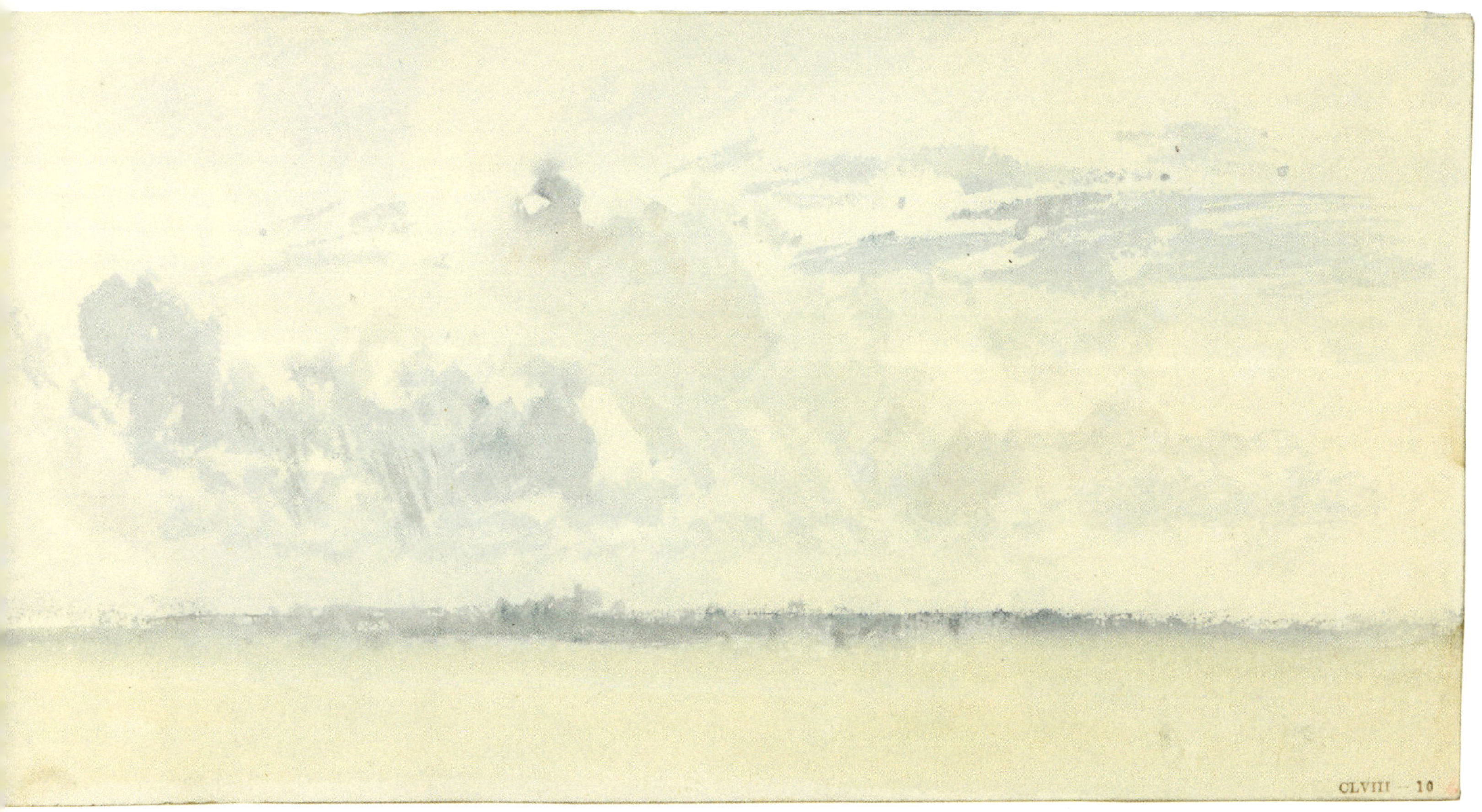

CLVIII – 10

CLVIII — 11

CLVIII — 12

CLVIII — 13

CLVIII — 14

CLVIII — 15

CLVIII — 16

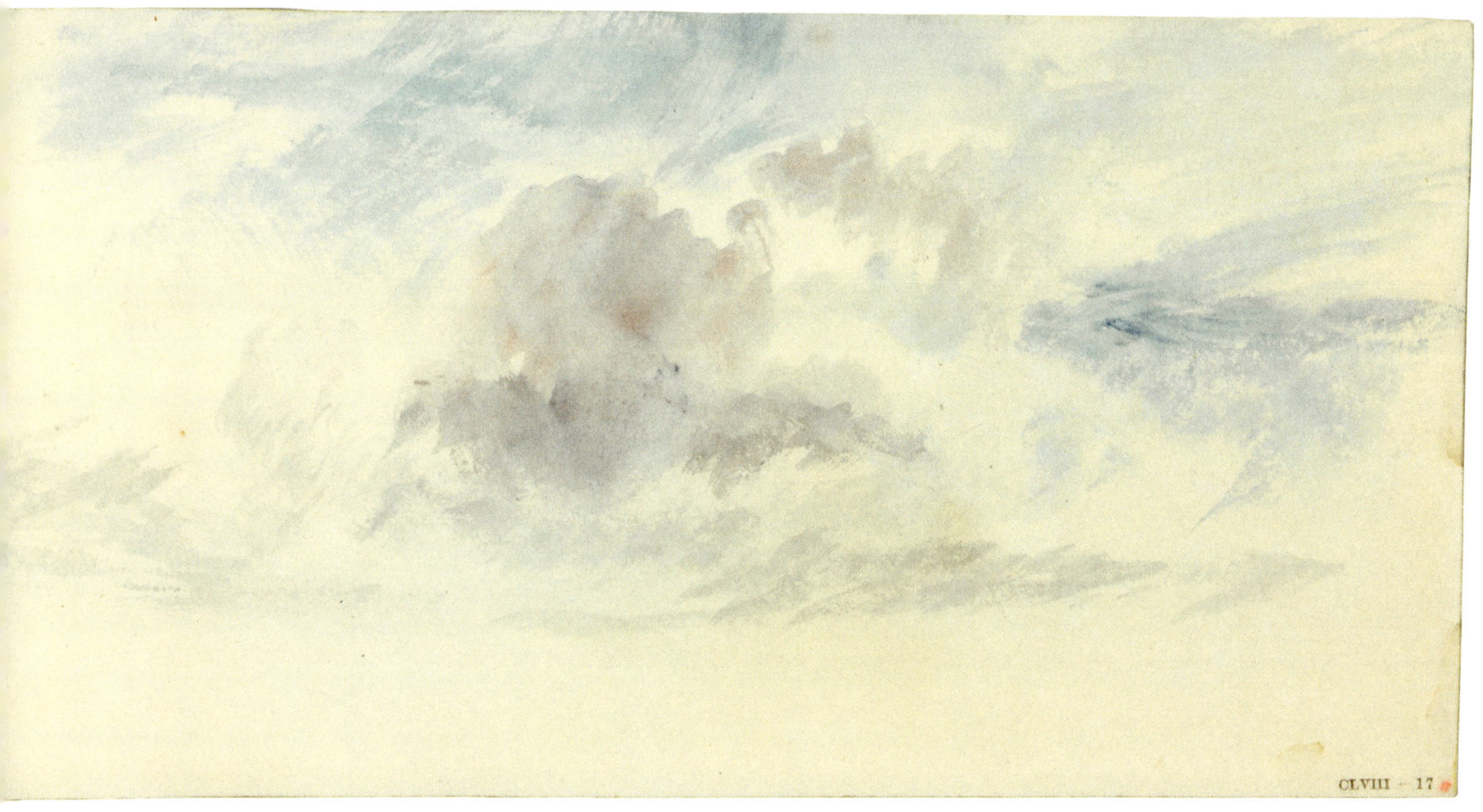

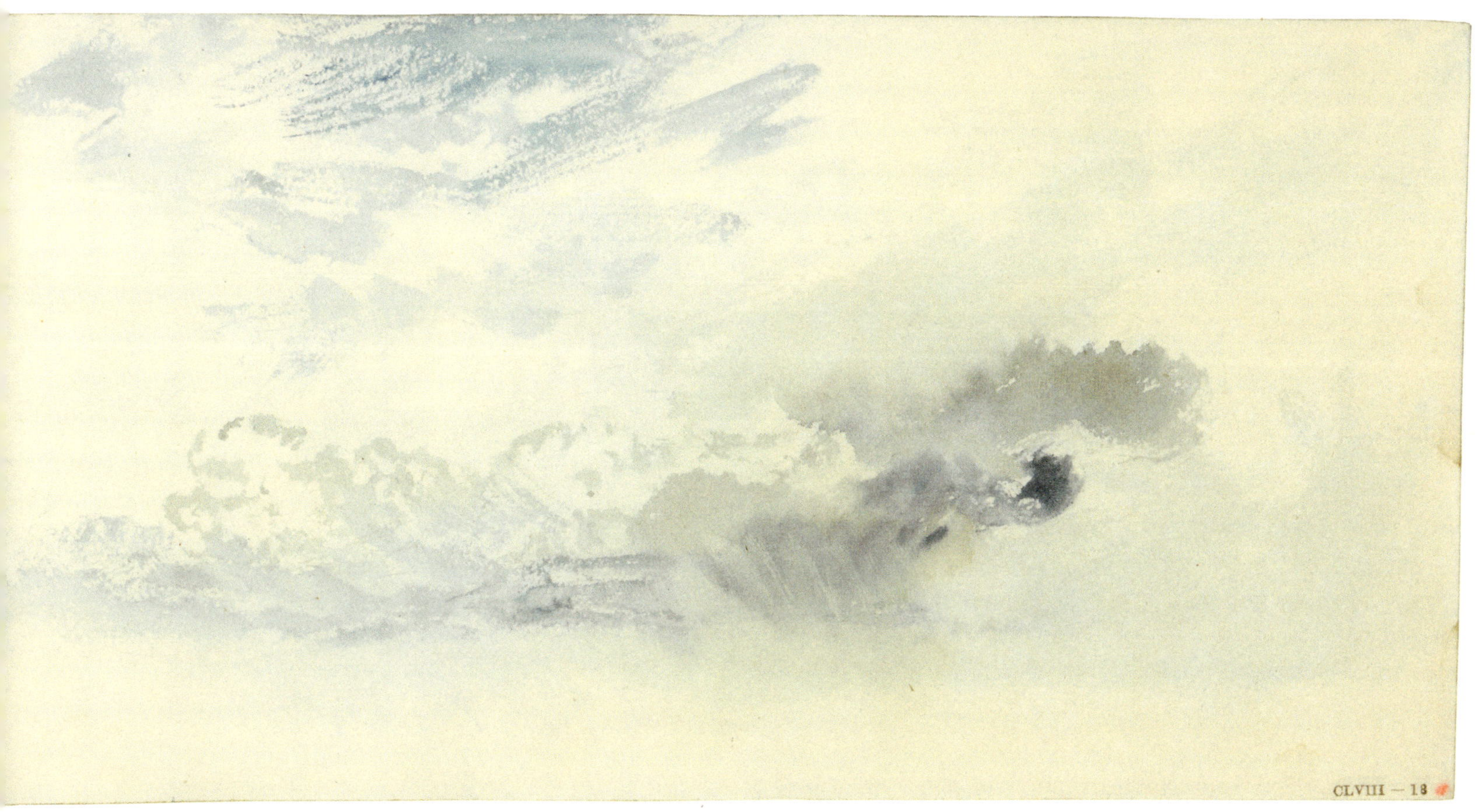

CLVIII — 13

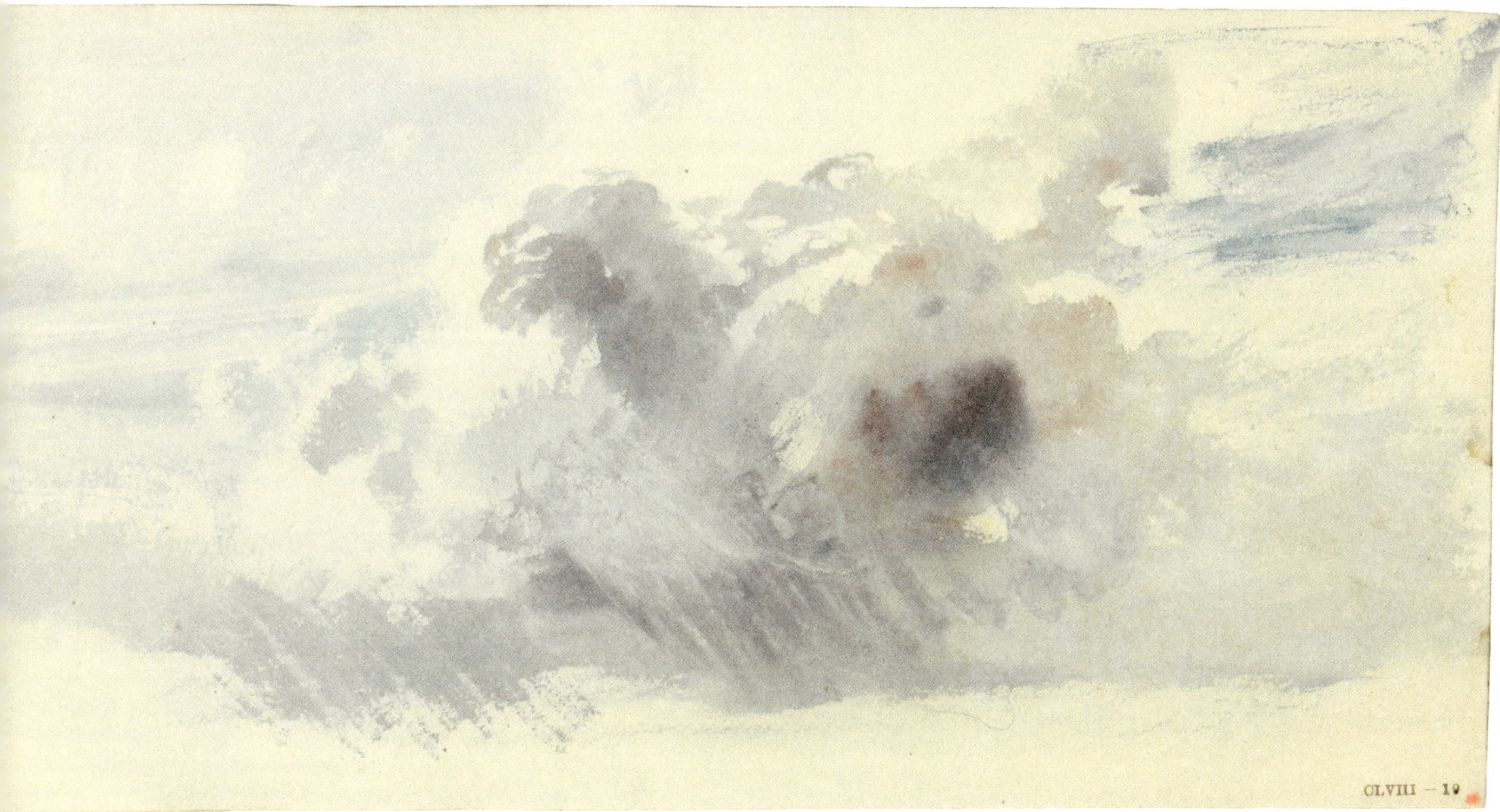

CLVIII – 19

CLVIII – 20

CLVIII — 21

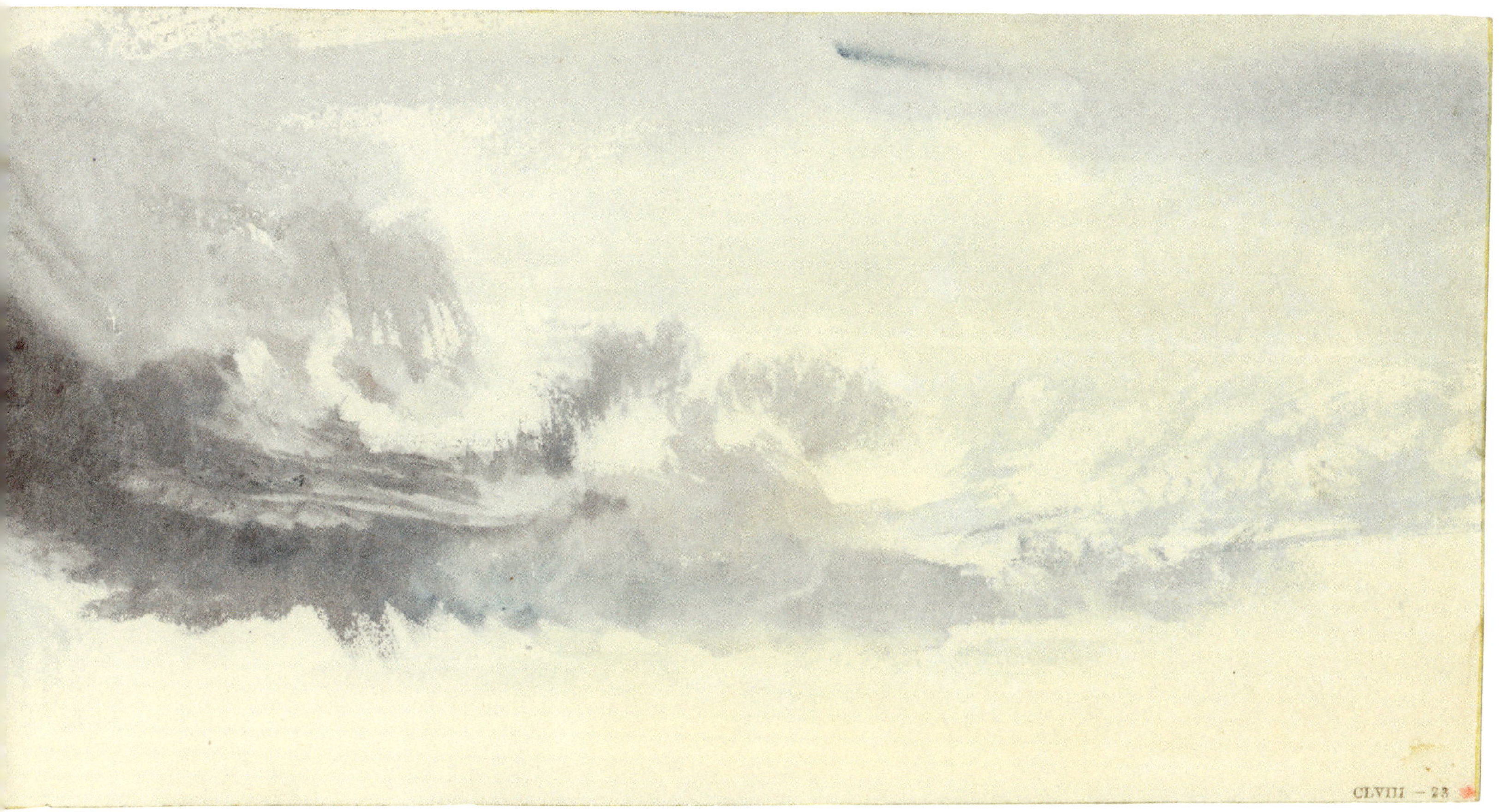

CLVIII — 23

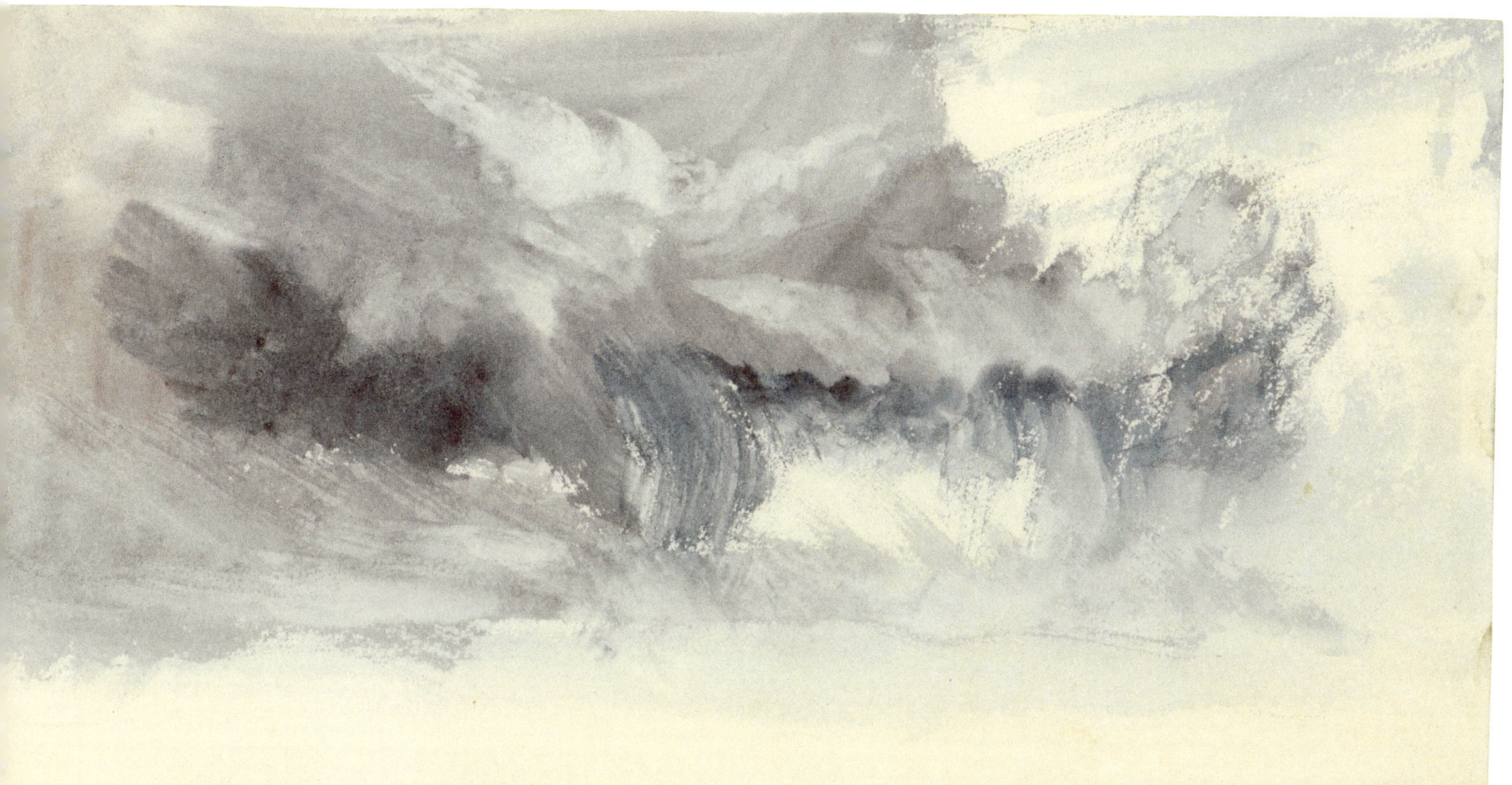

CLVIII — 24

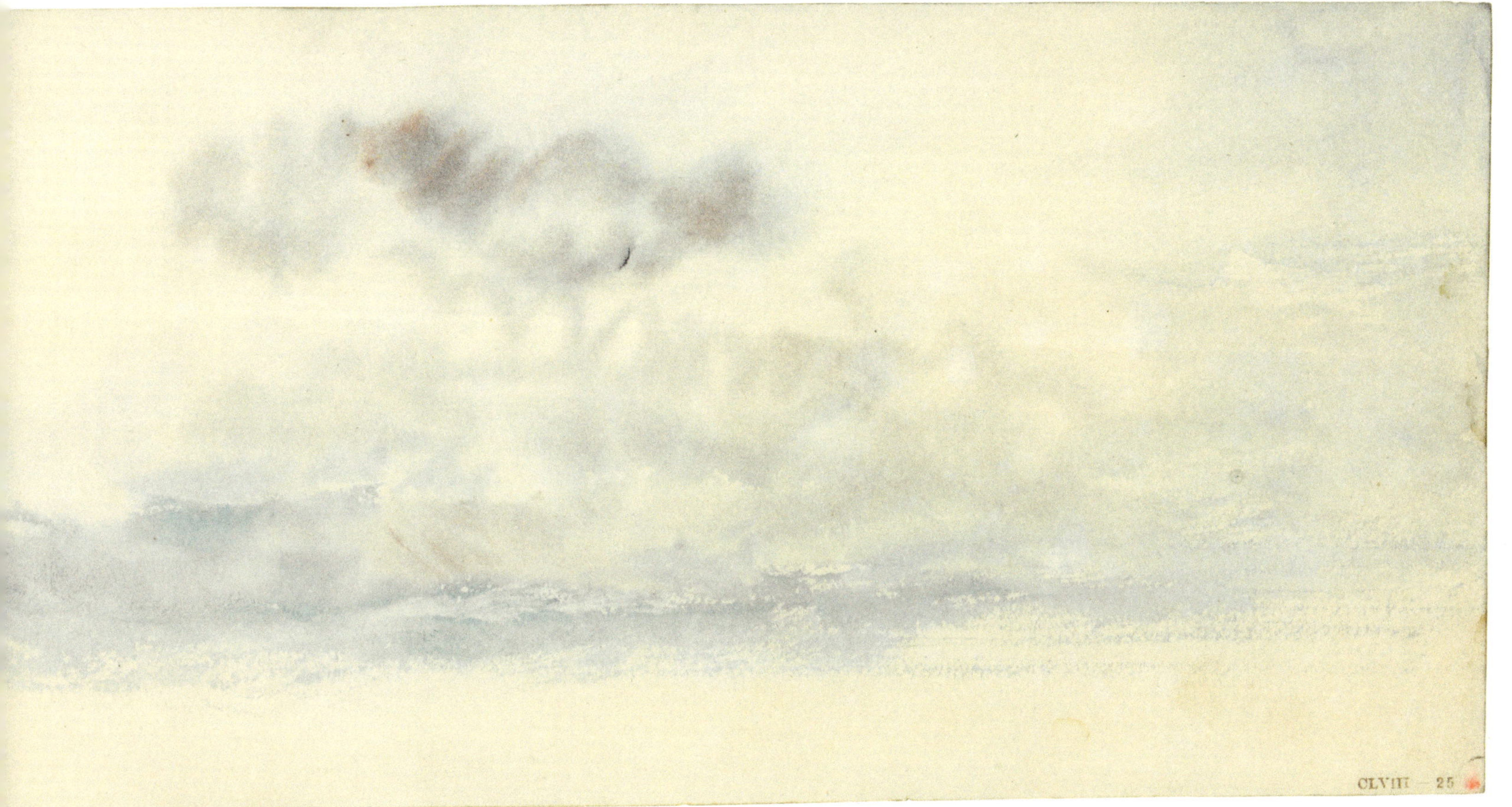

CLVIII — 26

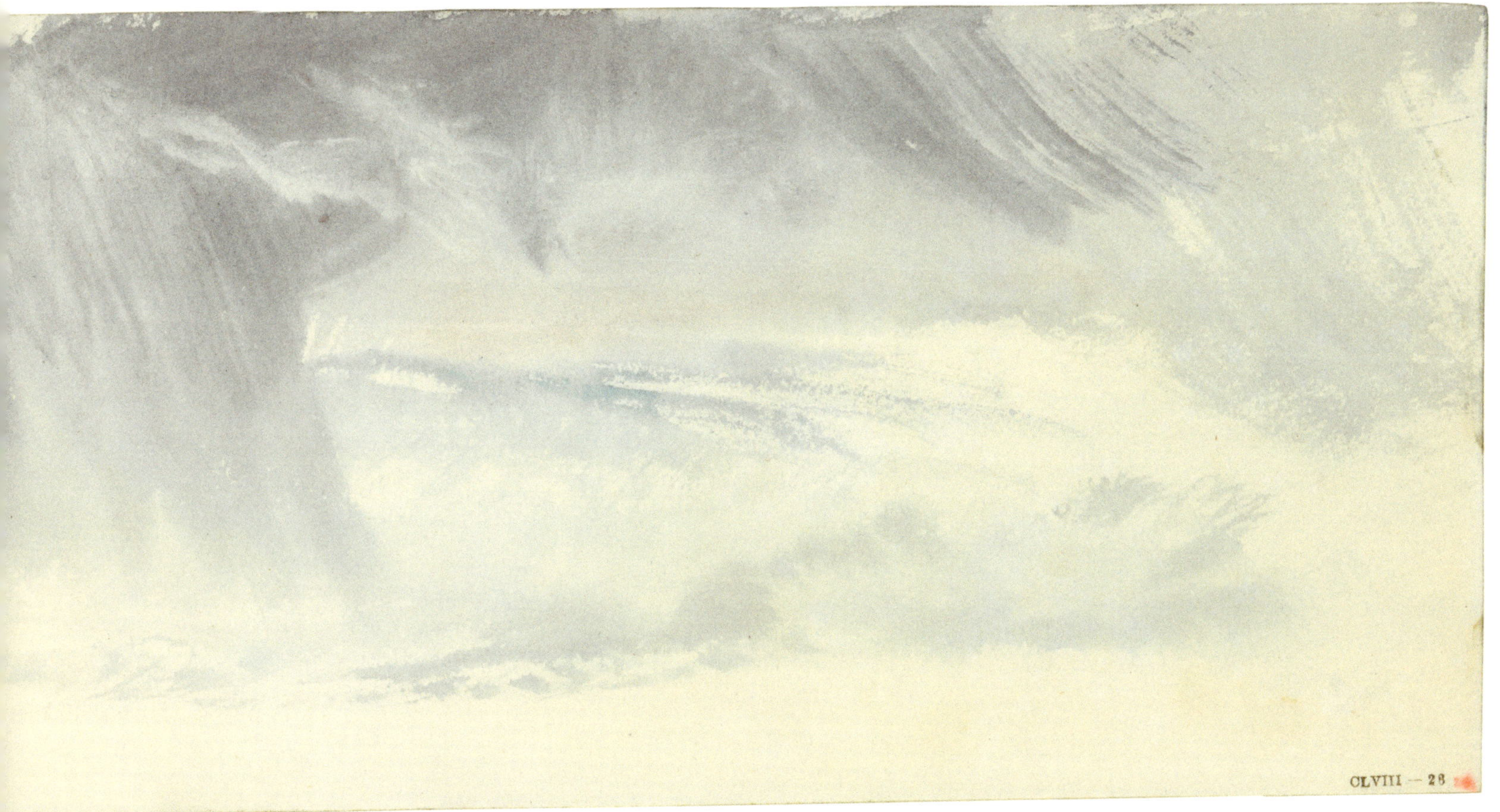
CLVIII — 26

CLVIII — 29

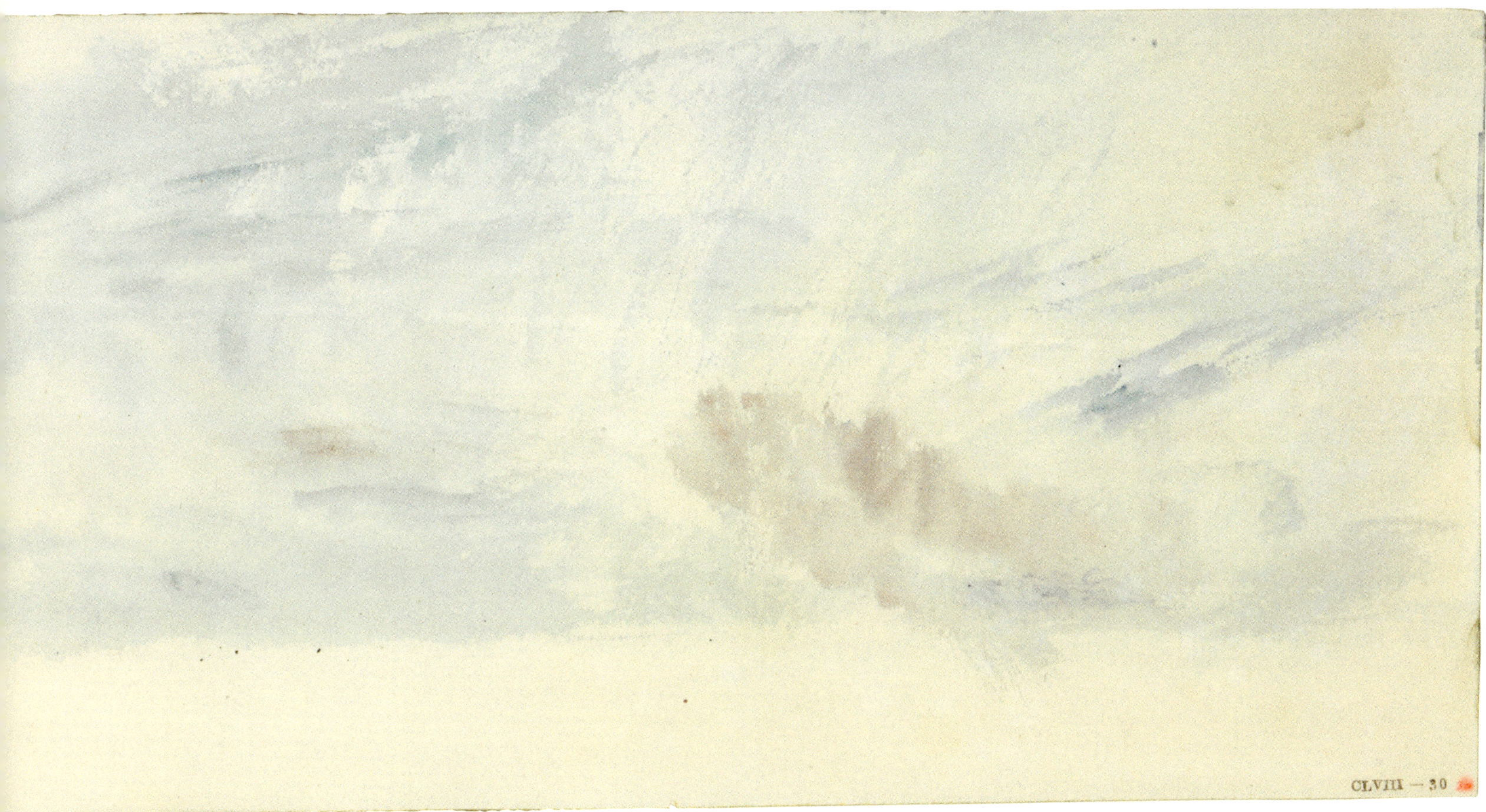

CLVIII — 30

CLVIII — 31

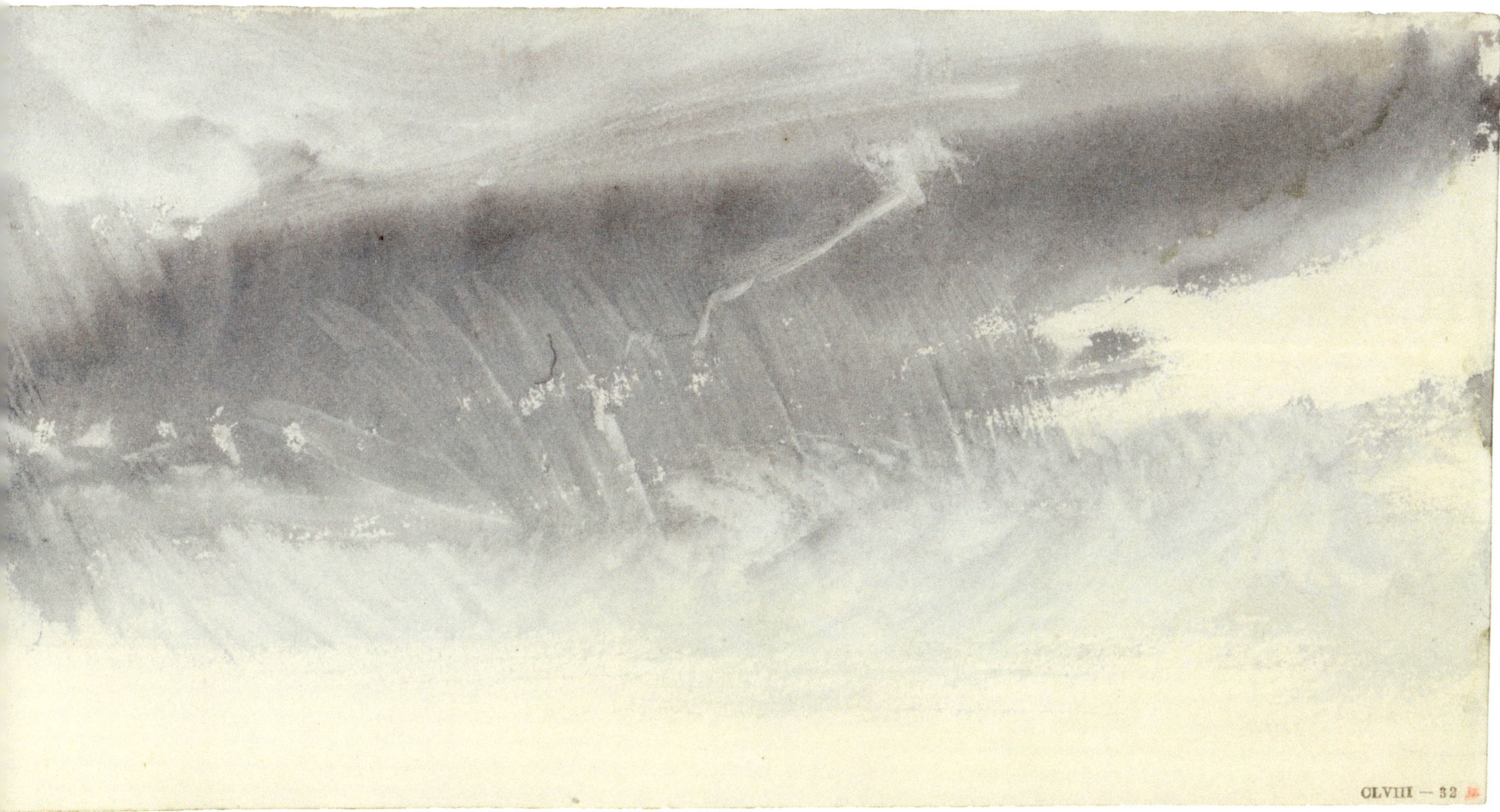

CLVIII — 32

CLVIII — 33

.CLVIII — 34

CLVIII - 37

CLVIII — 38

CLVIII — 39

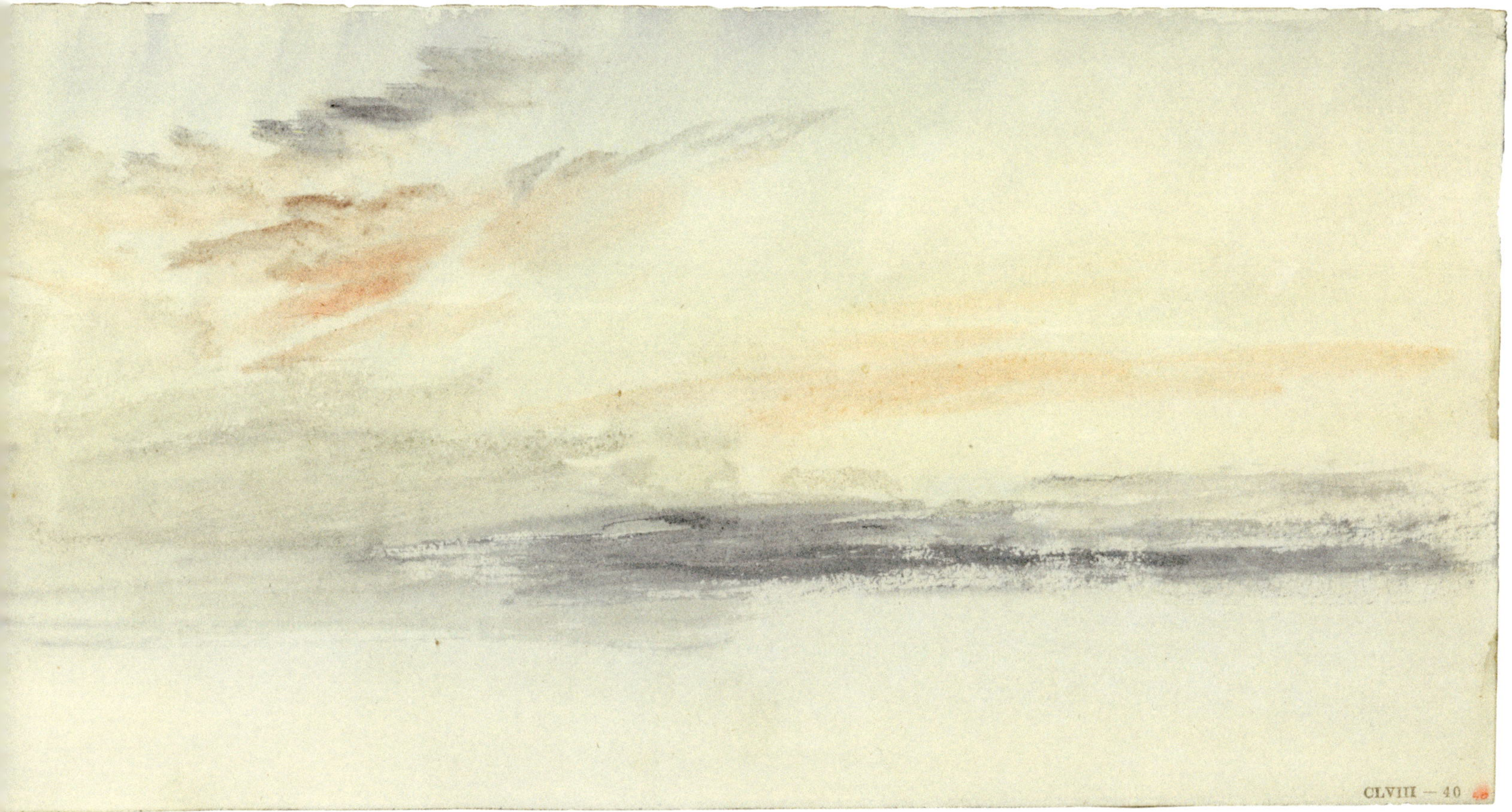

CLVIII — 40

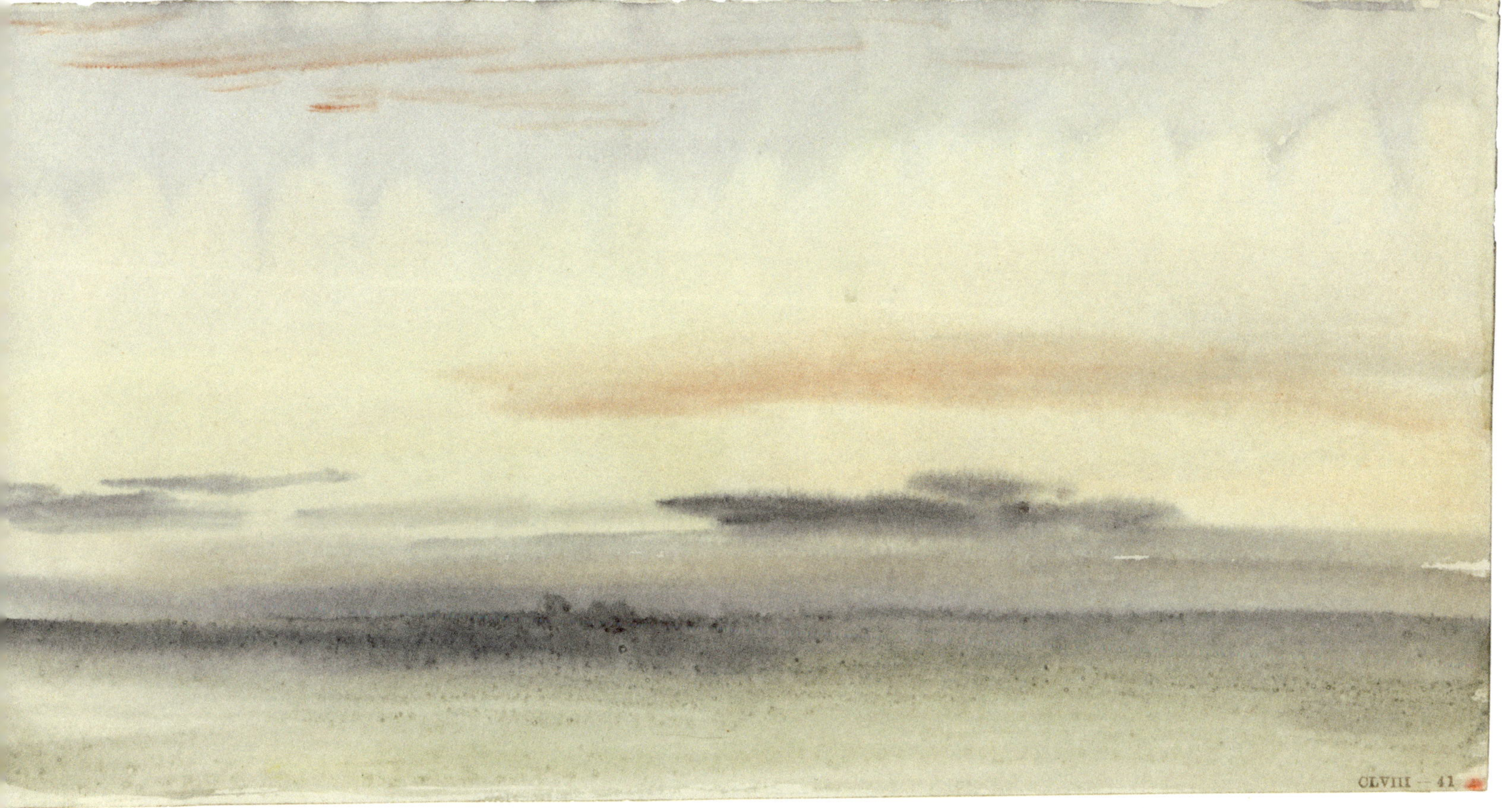
CLVIII — 41

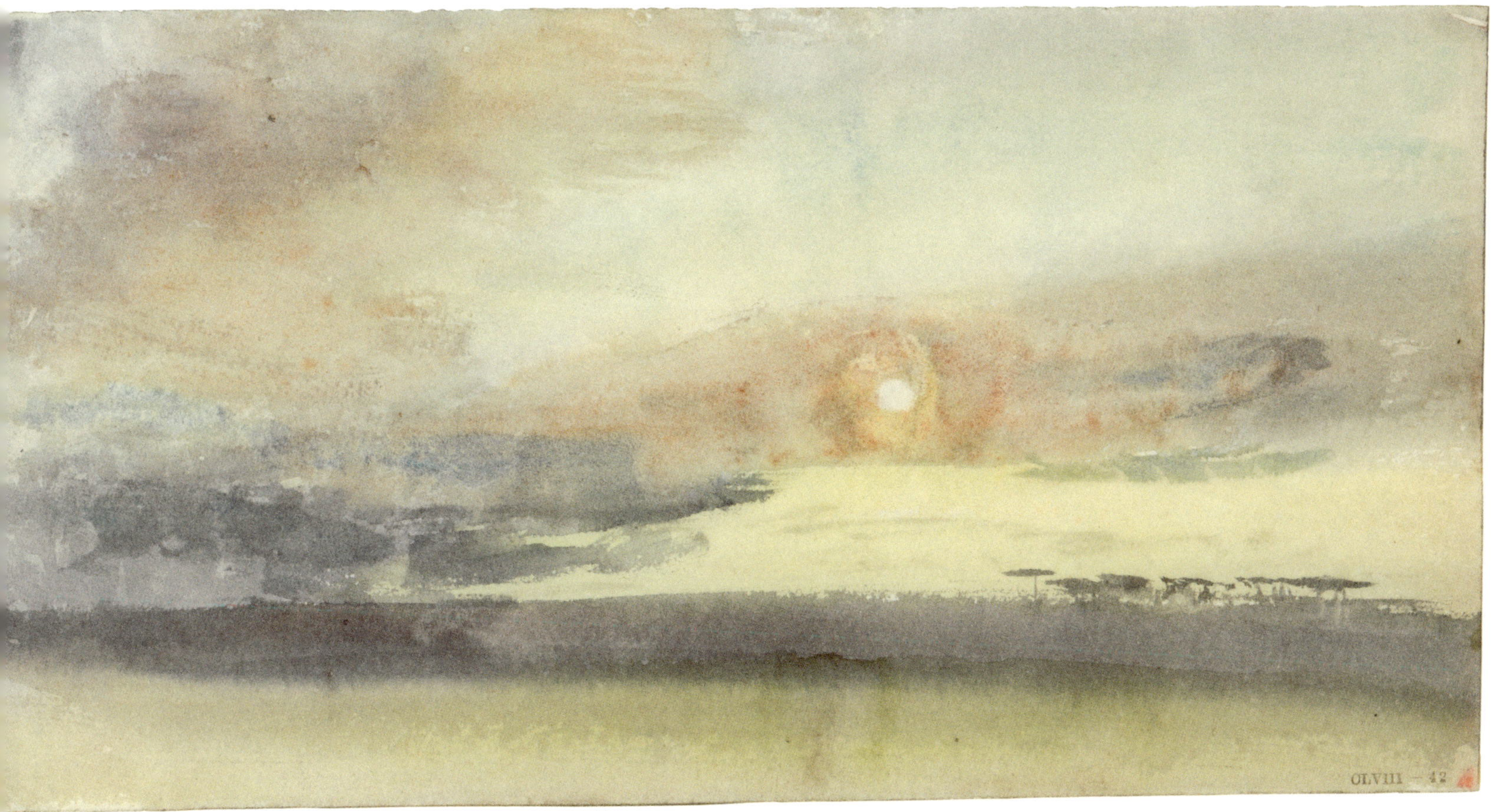
CLVIII — 42

CLVIII — 43

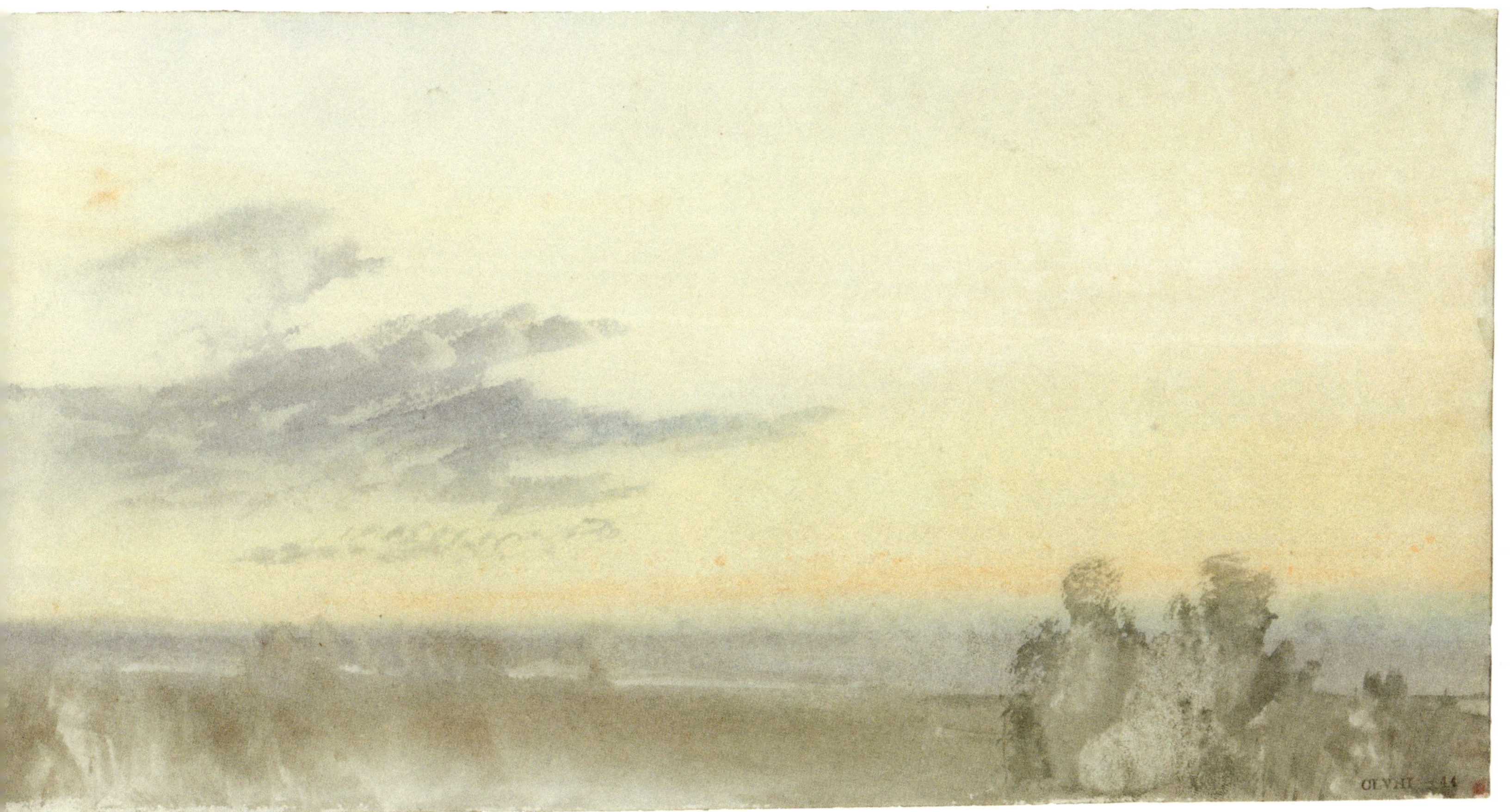

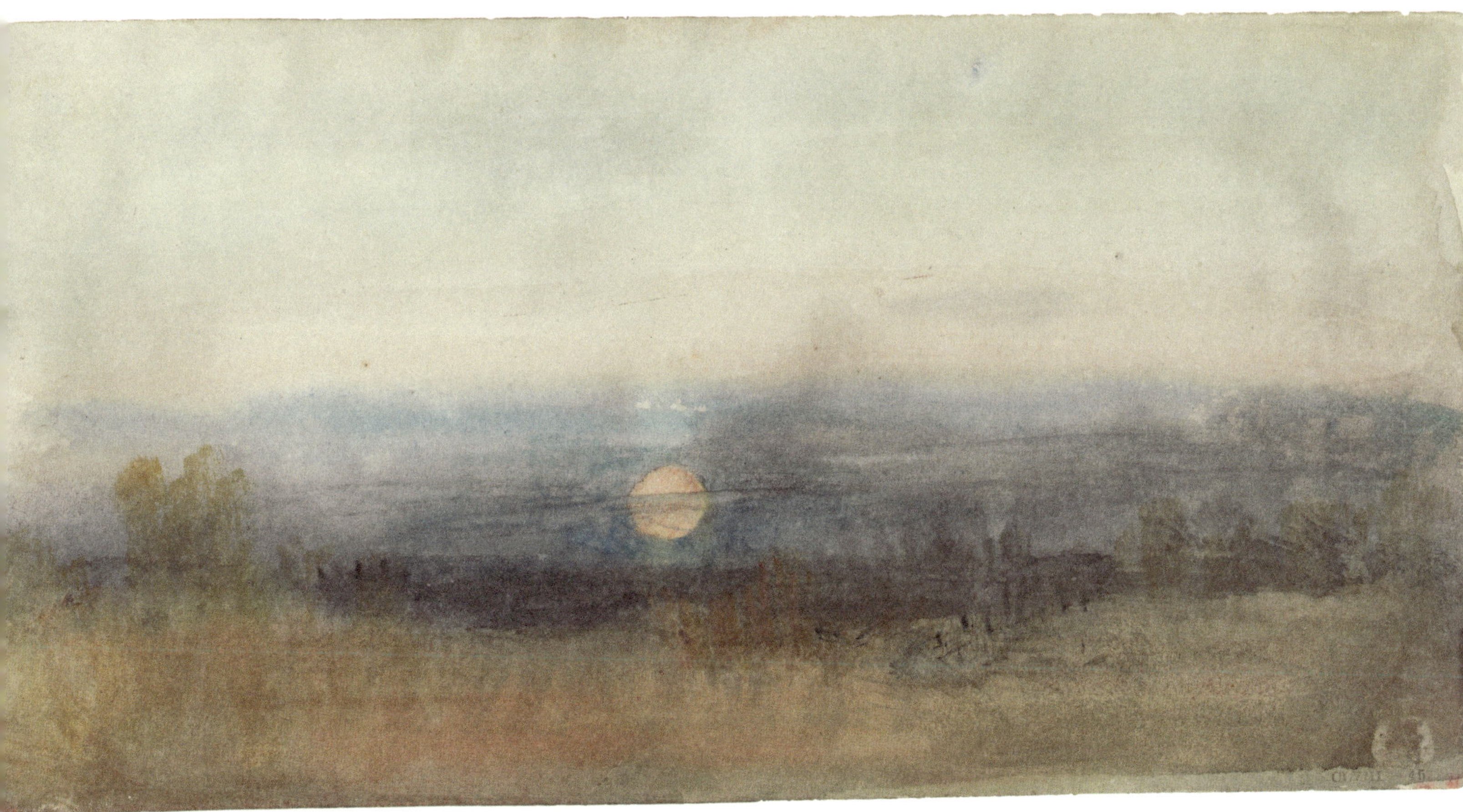

CLVIII — 47

CLVIII — 48

CLVIII – 49

CLVIII 50

CLVIII — 51

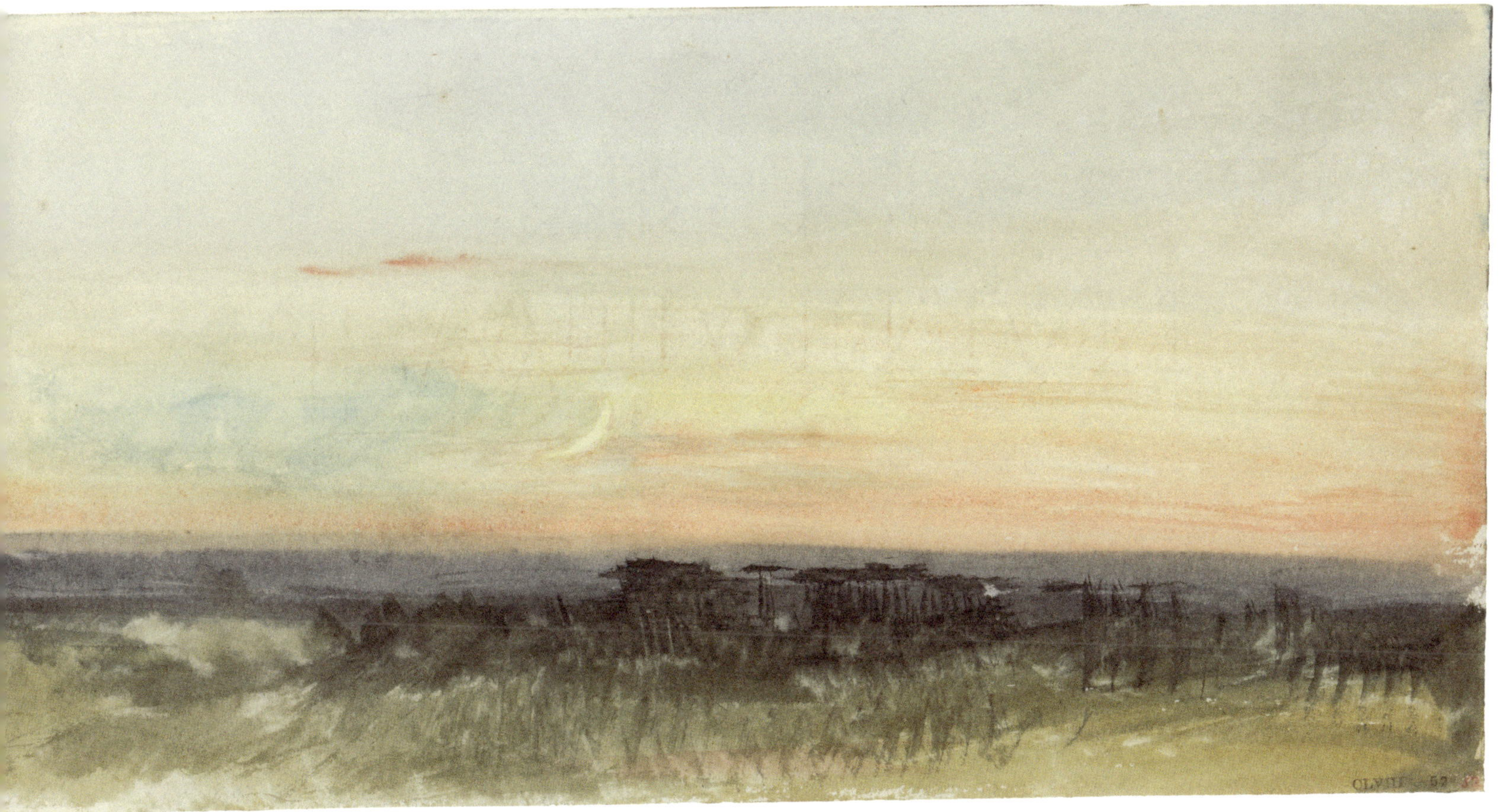

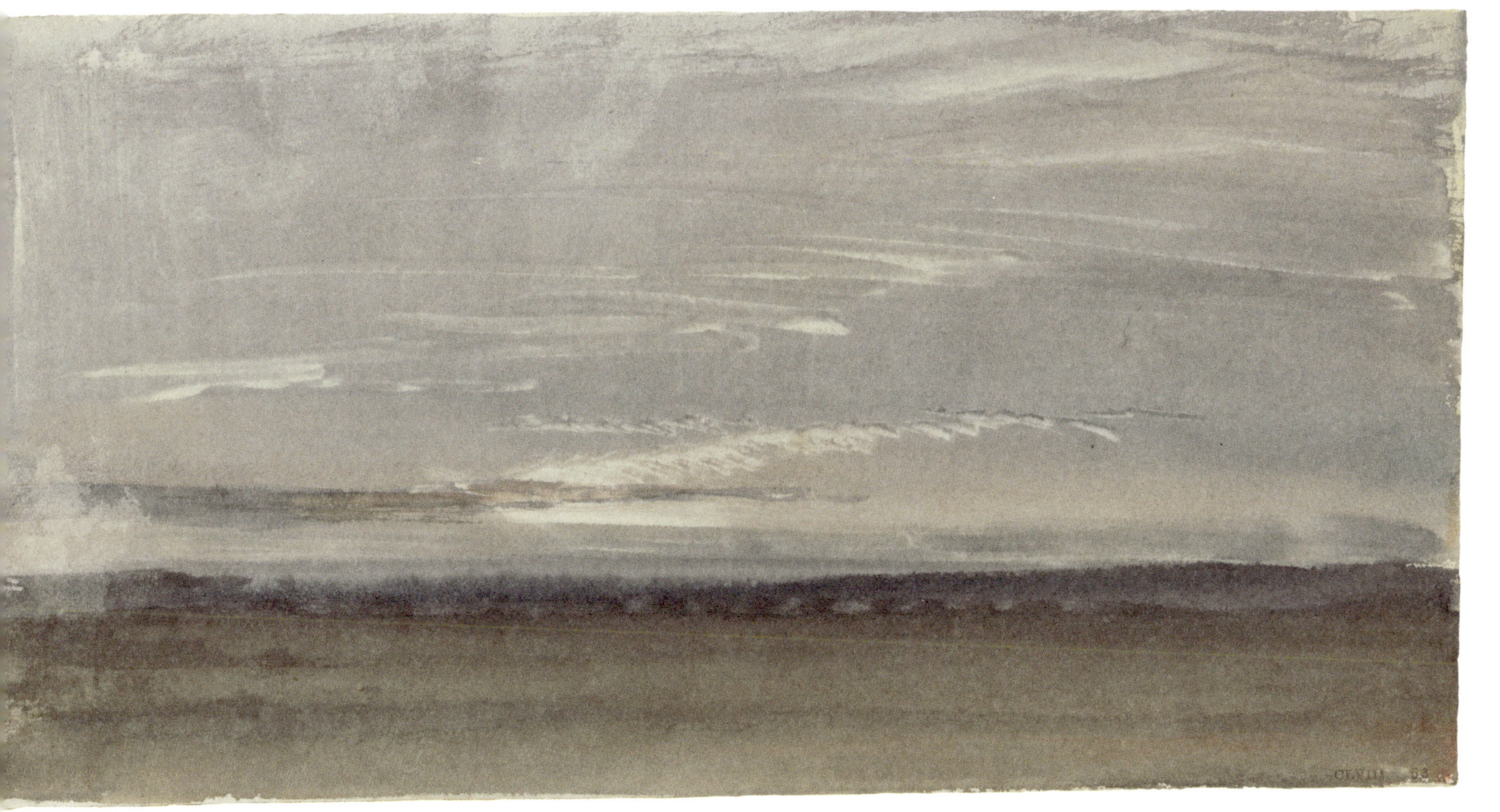

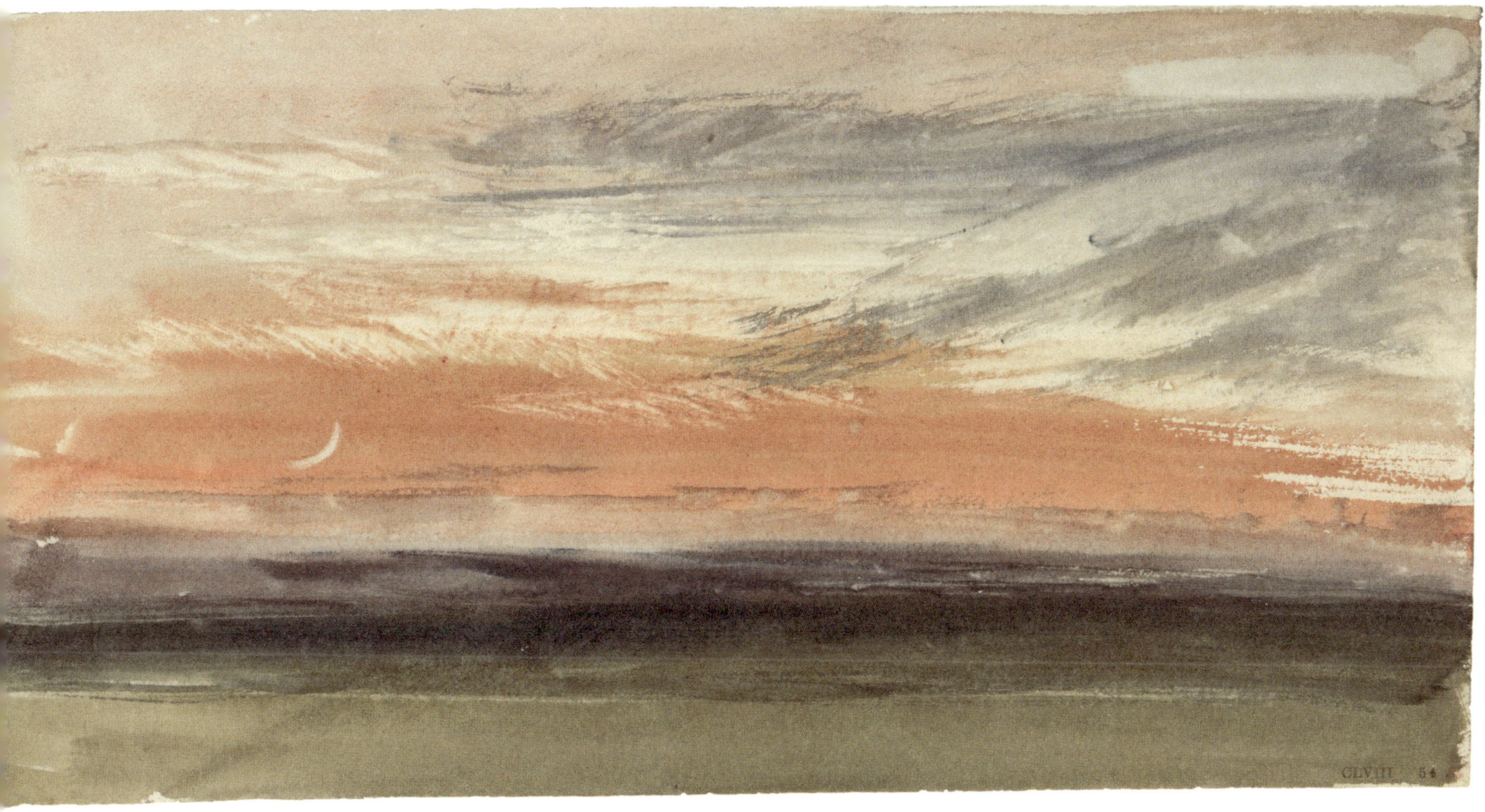
CLVIII 54

CLVIII — 55

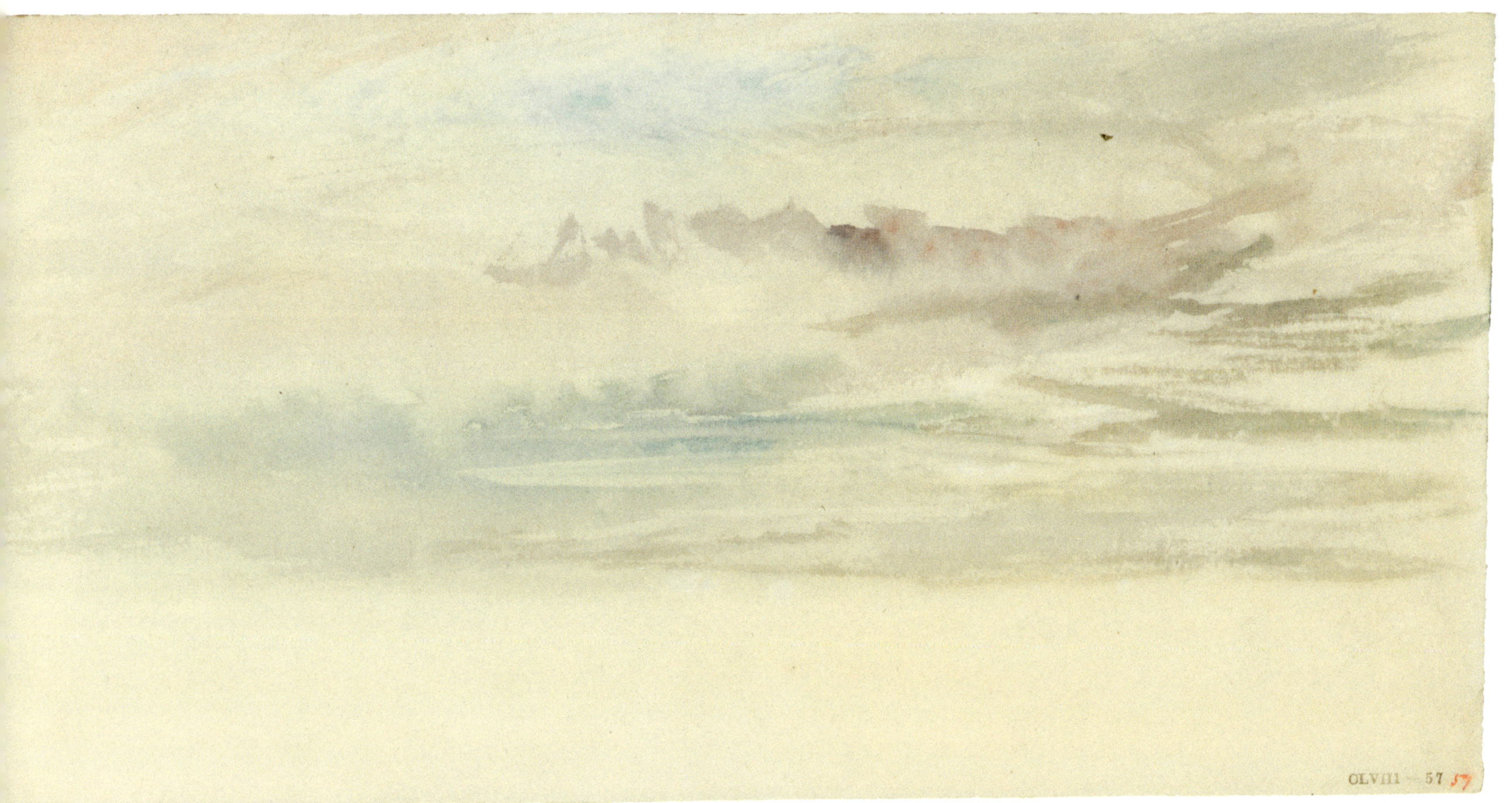
CLVIII – 57 57

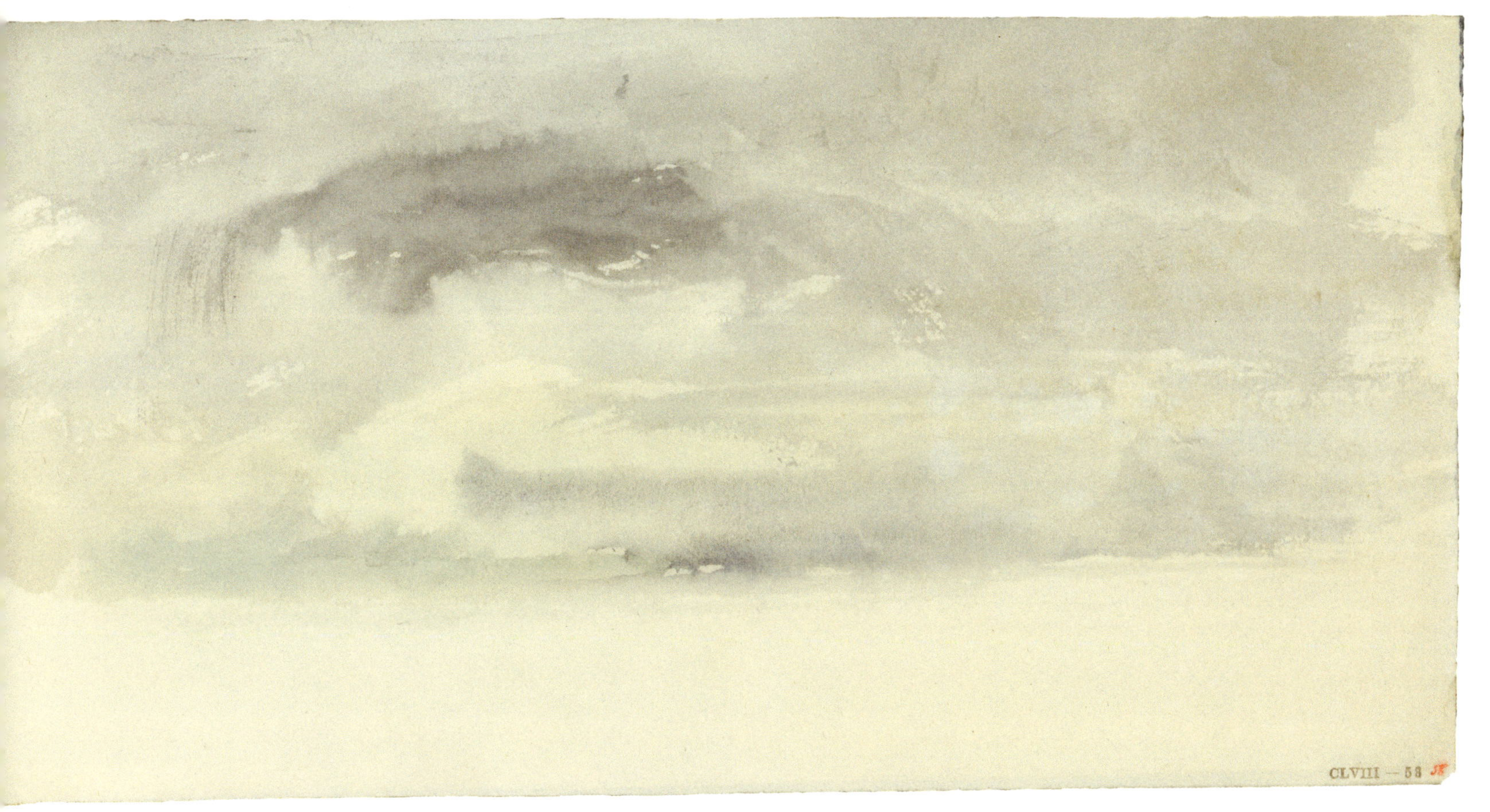
CLVIII — 58

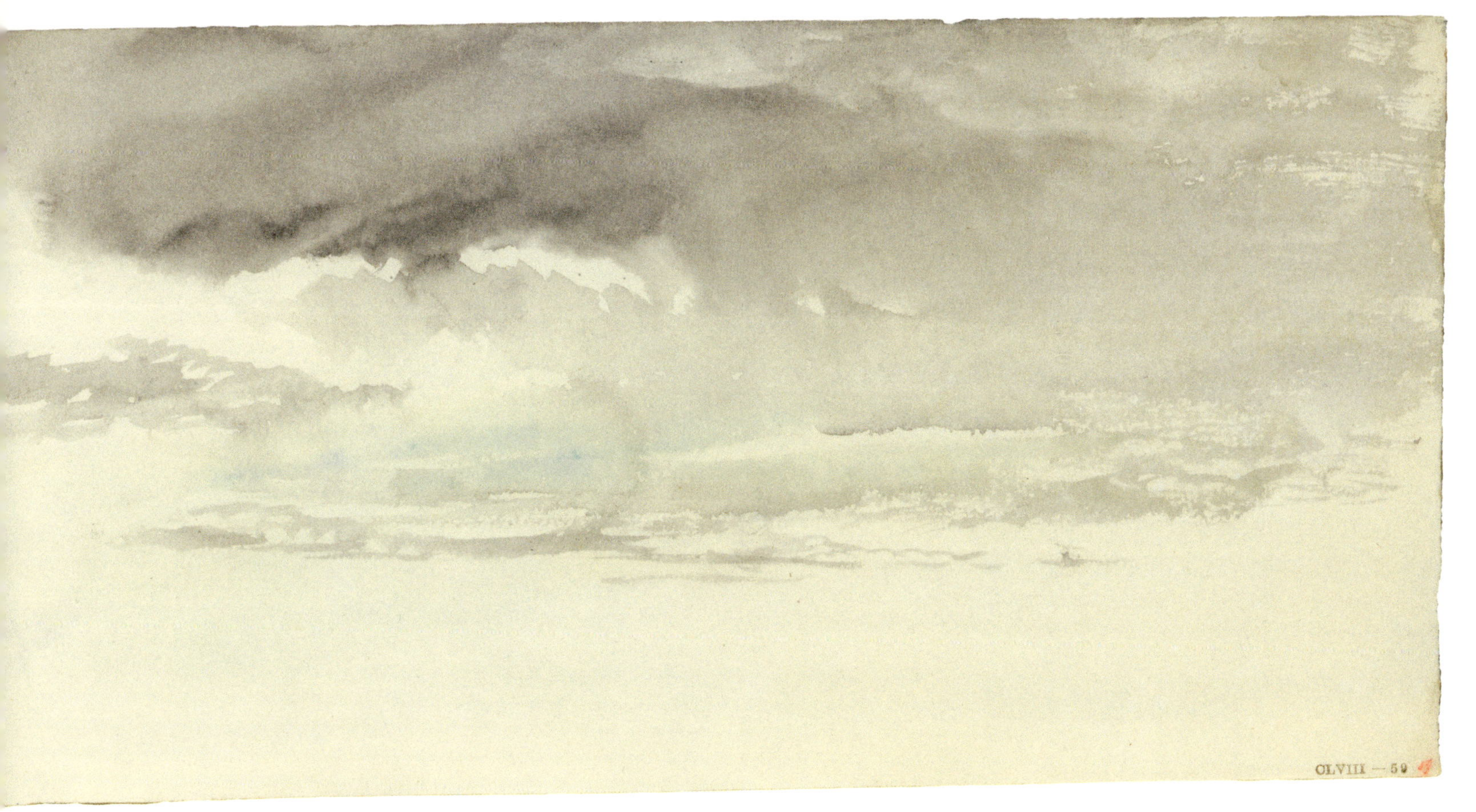
CLVIII — 59

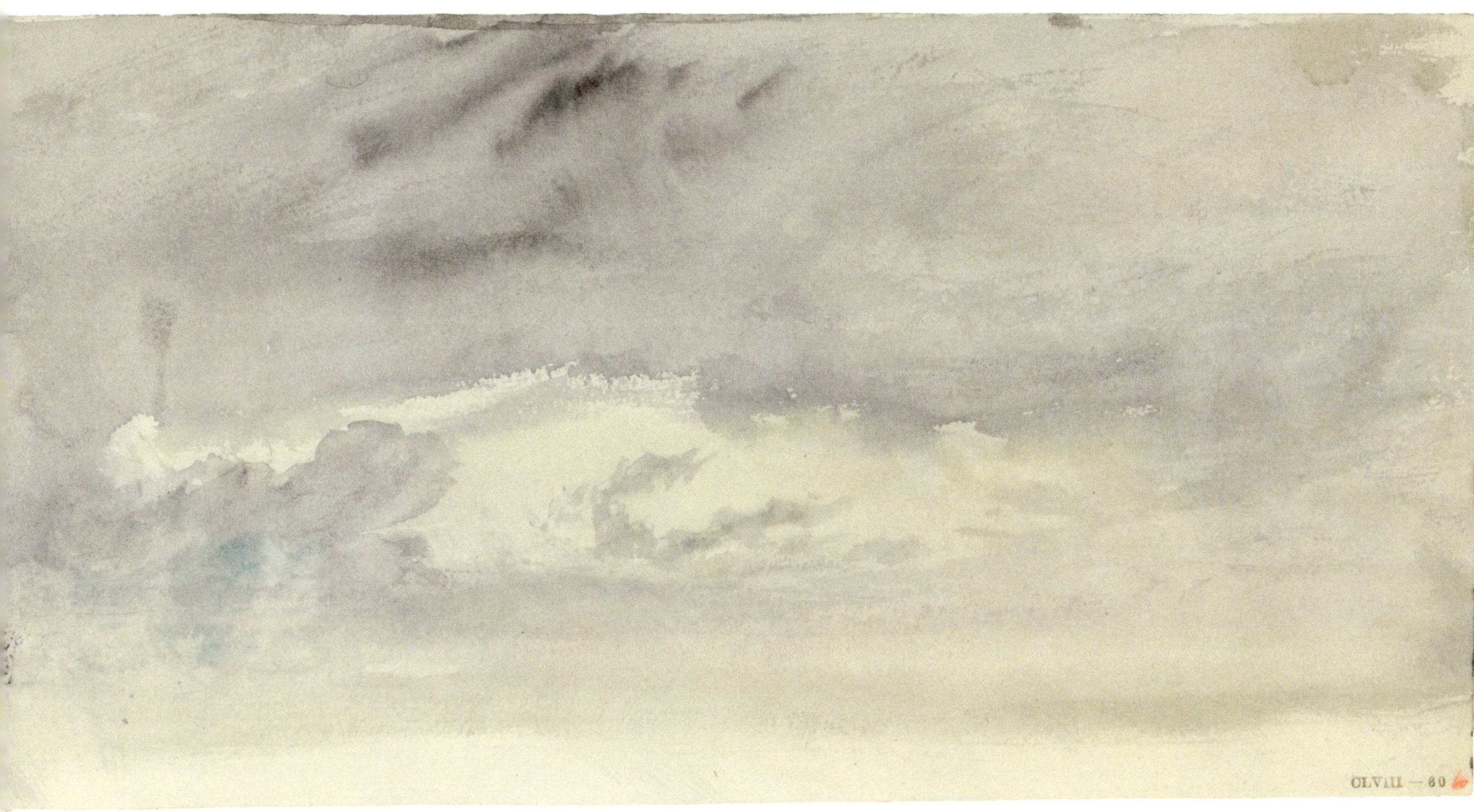

CLVIII — 60

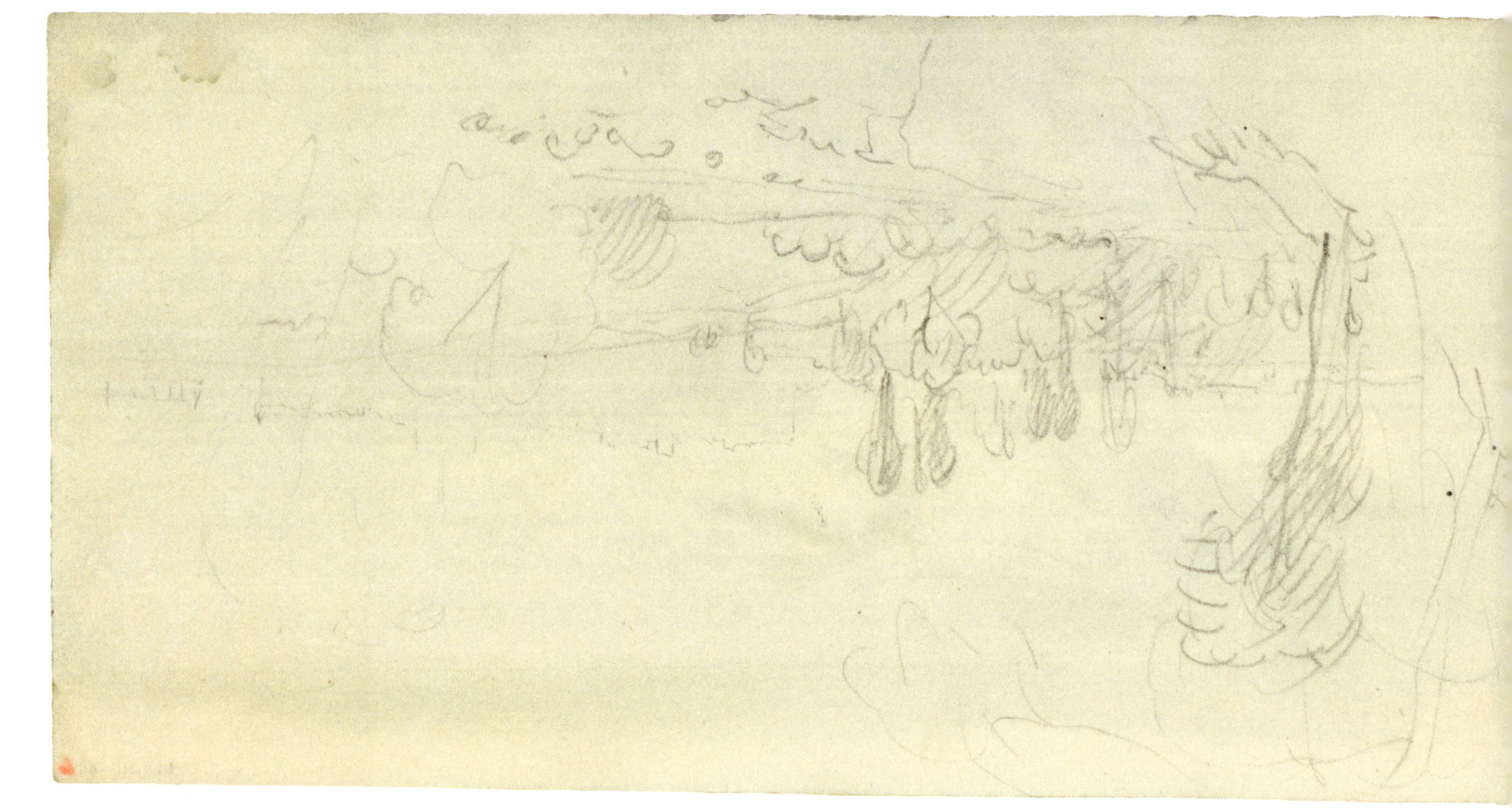

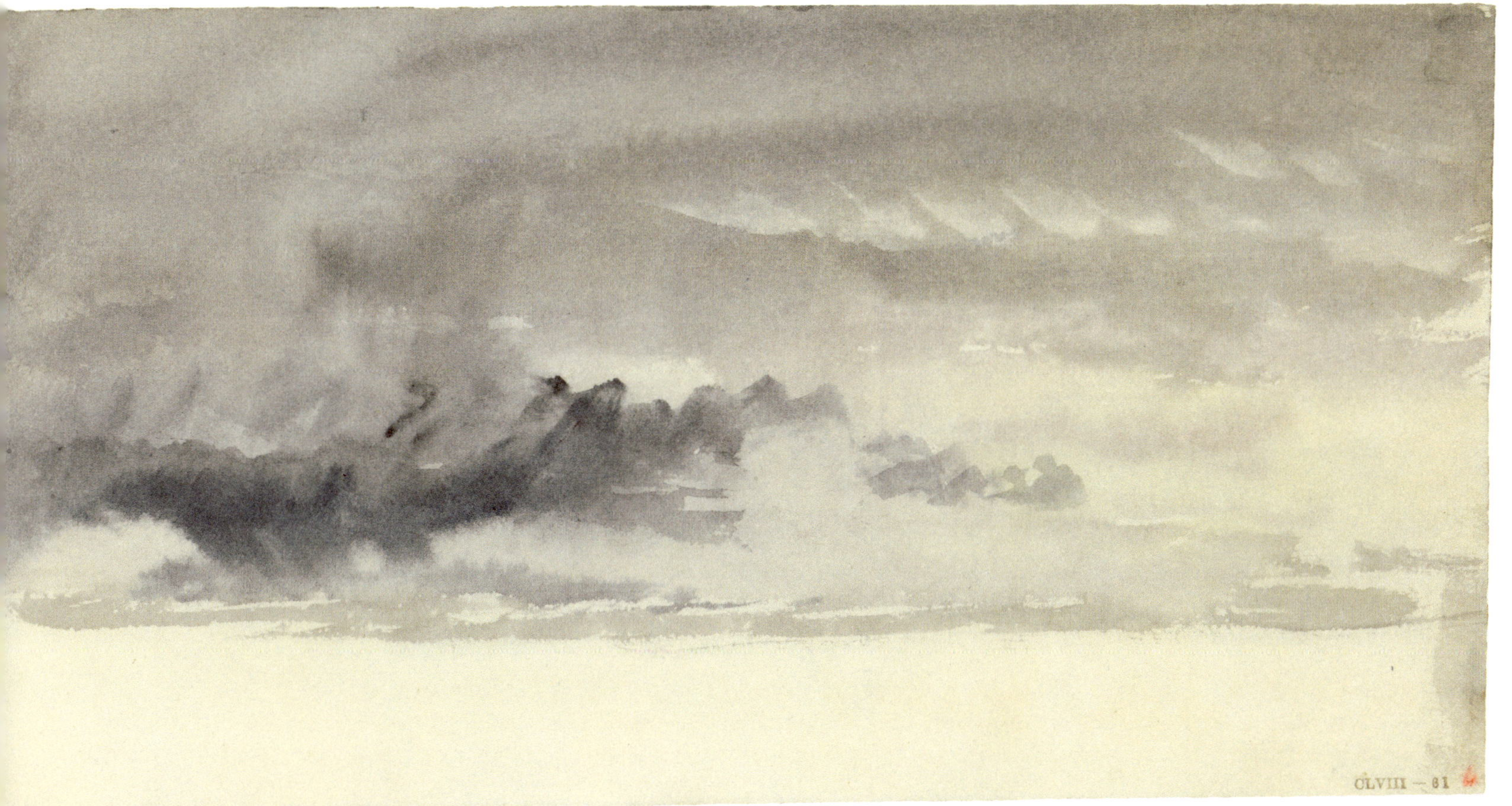

CLVIII — 81

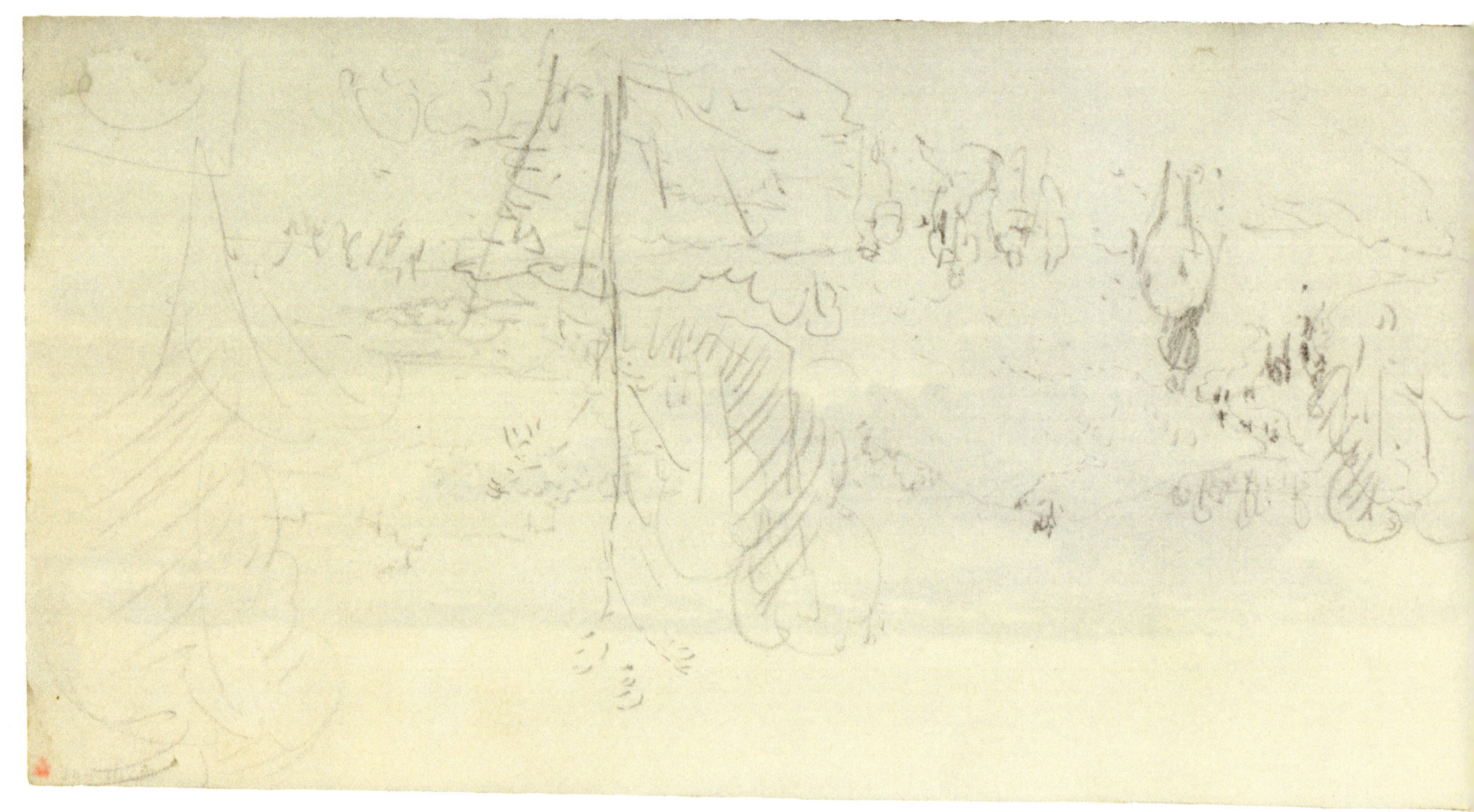

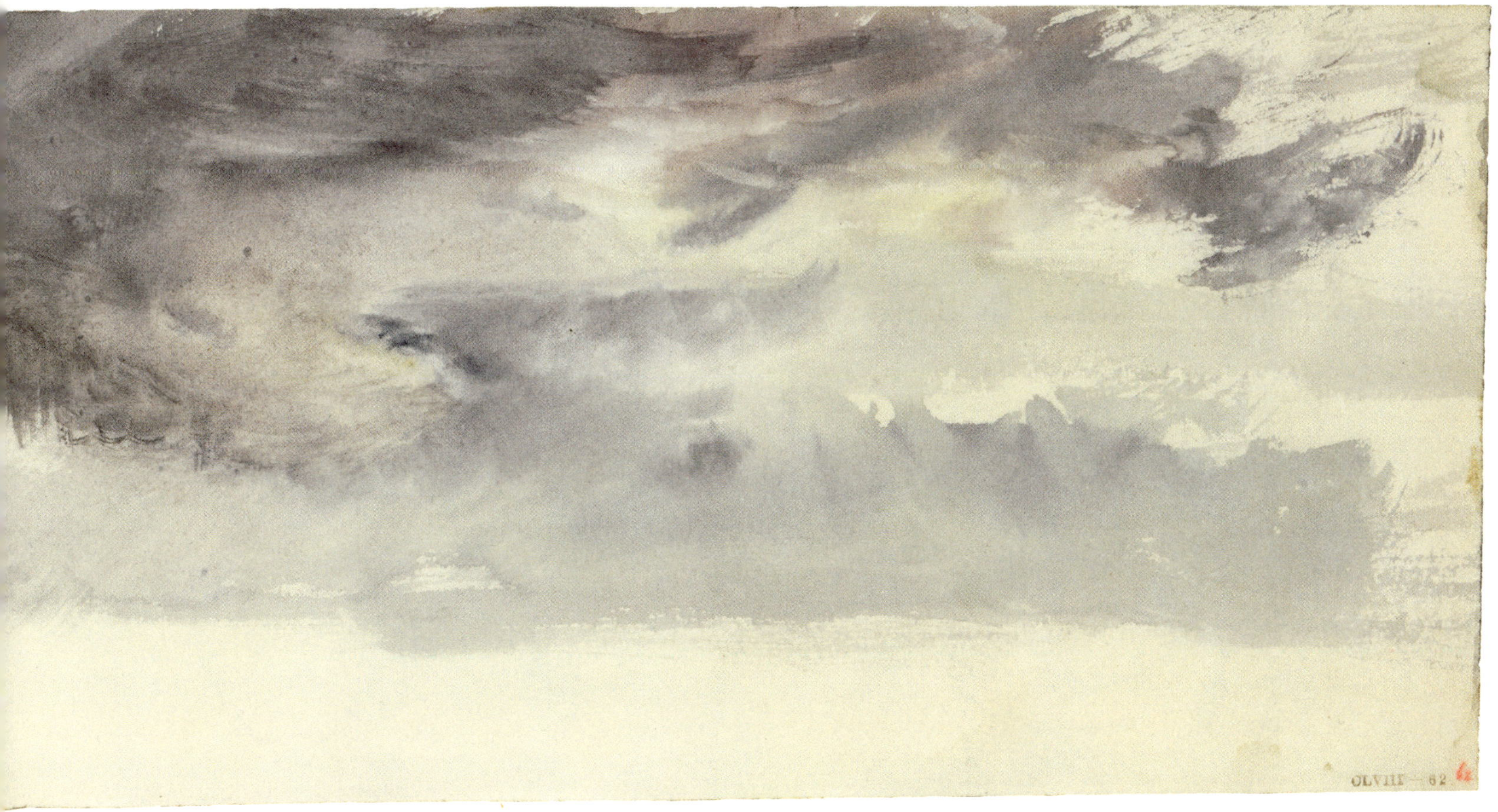
CLVIII — 62

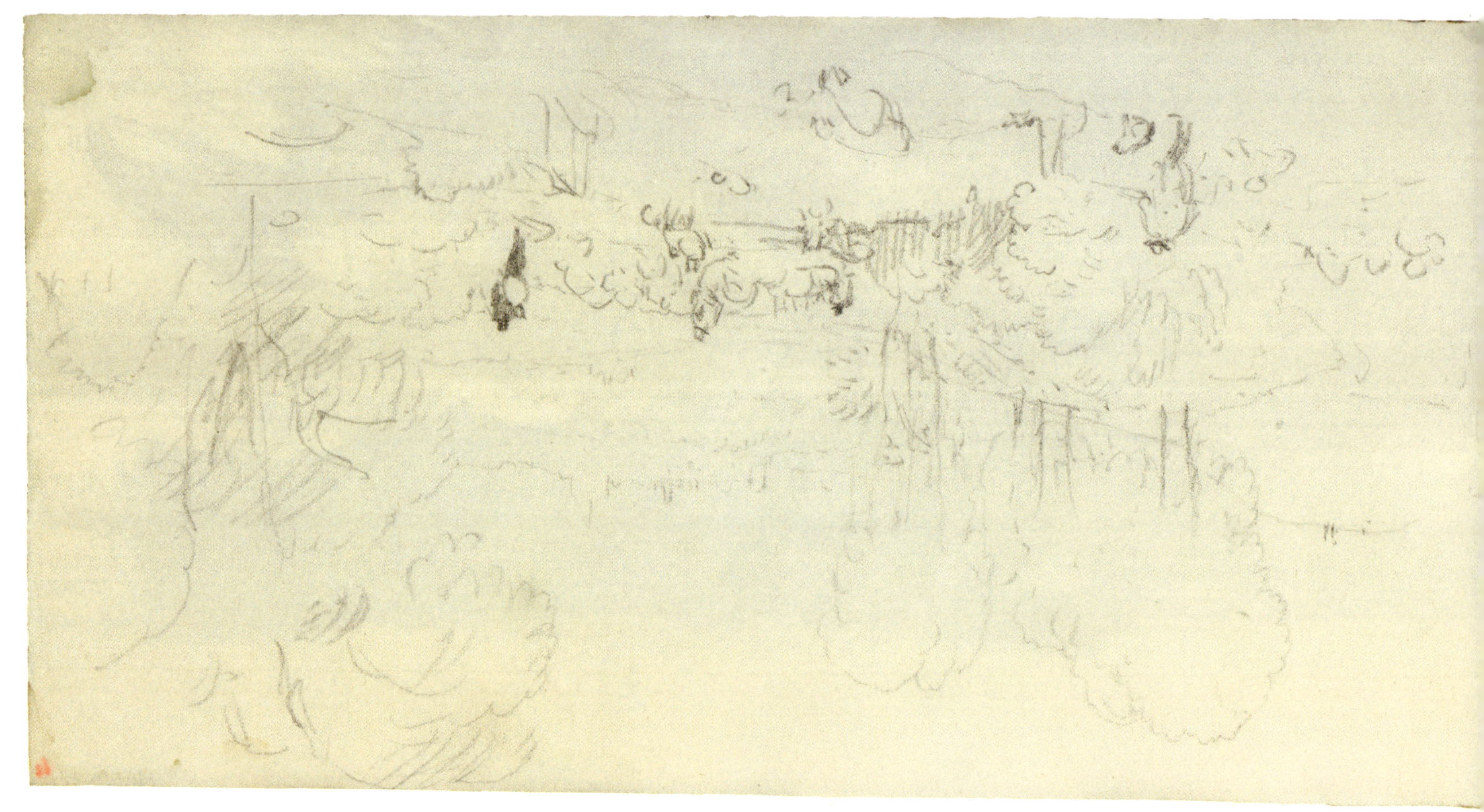

CLVIII — 63

CLVIII — 64

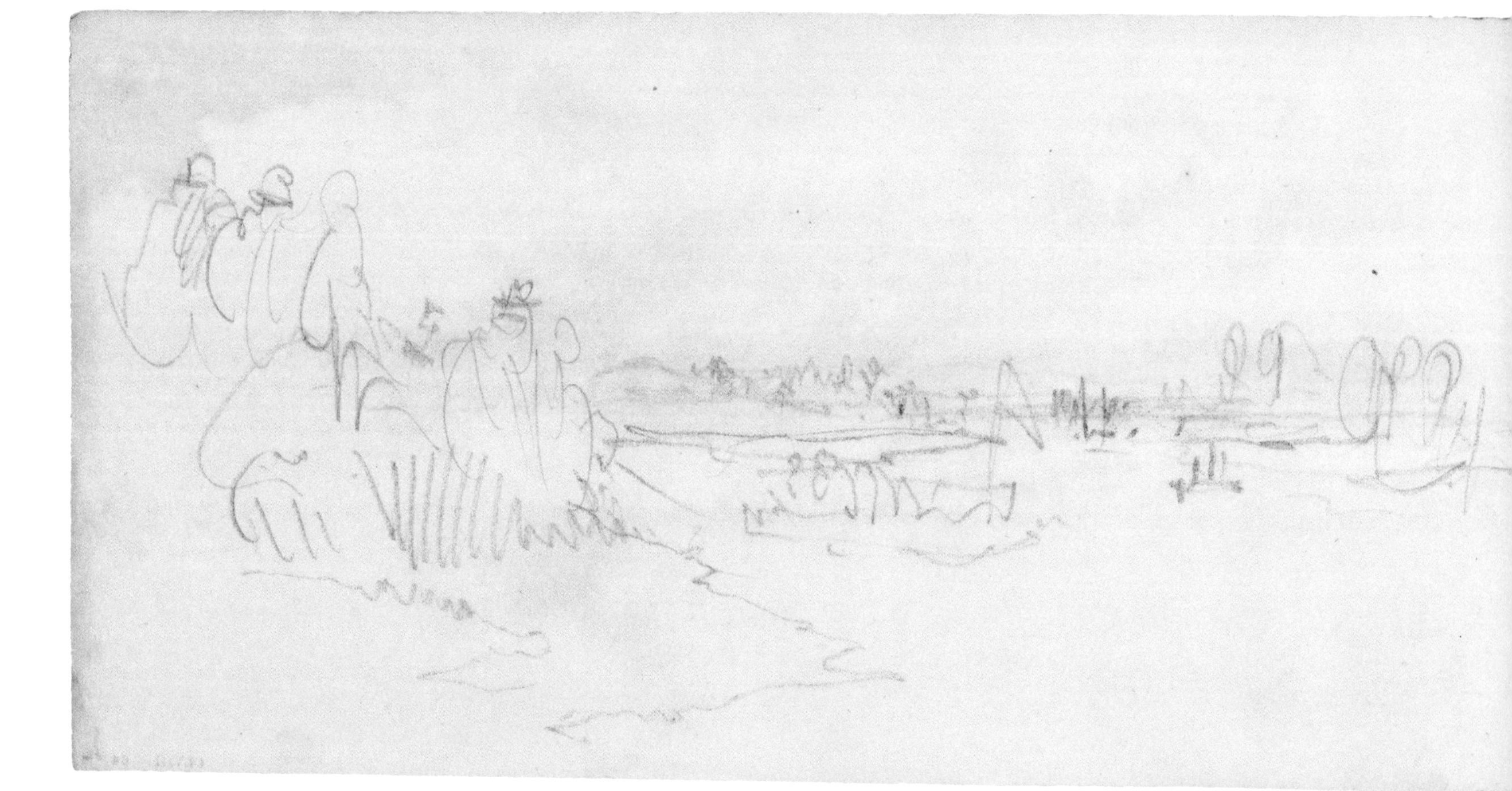

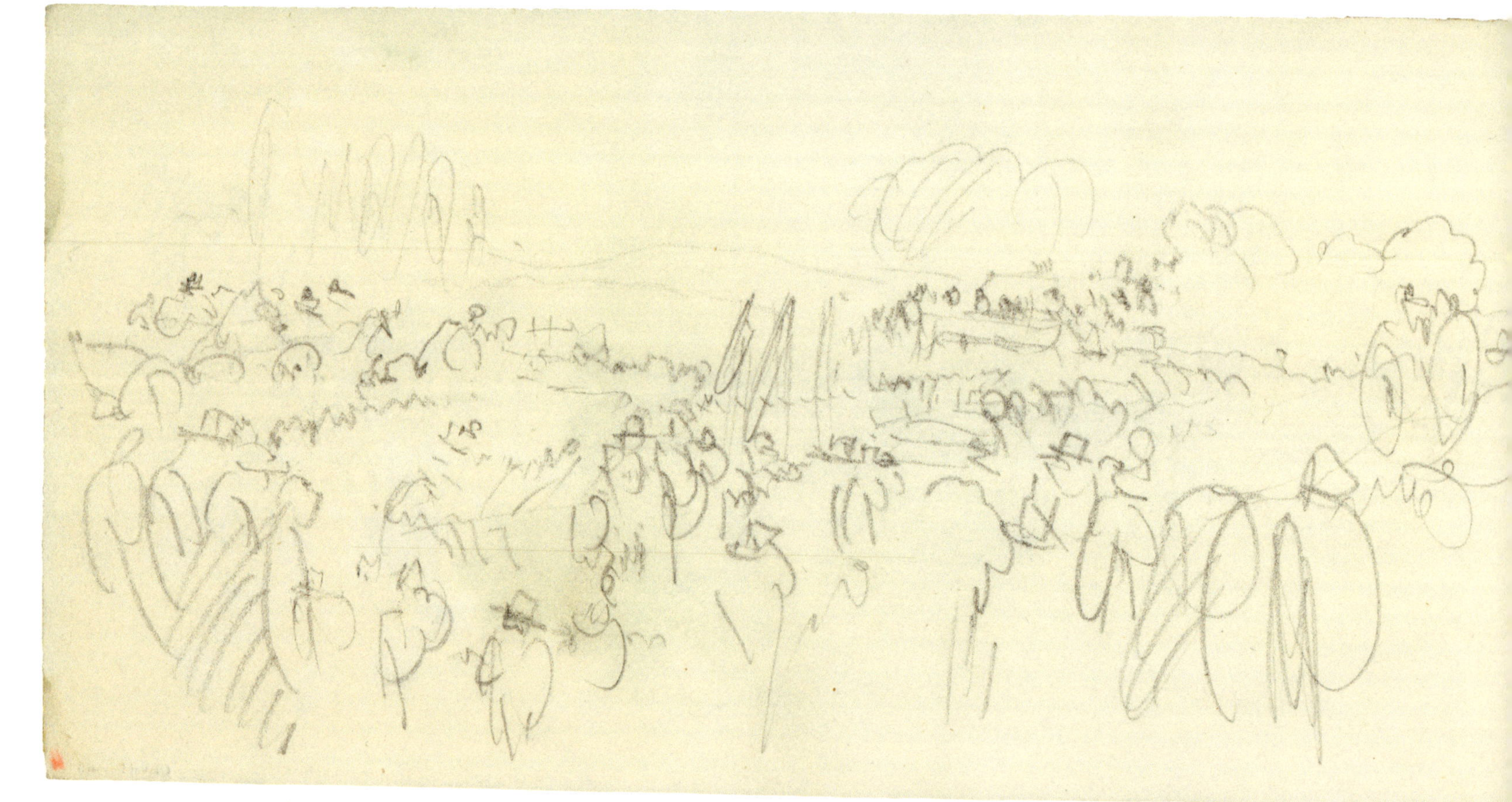

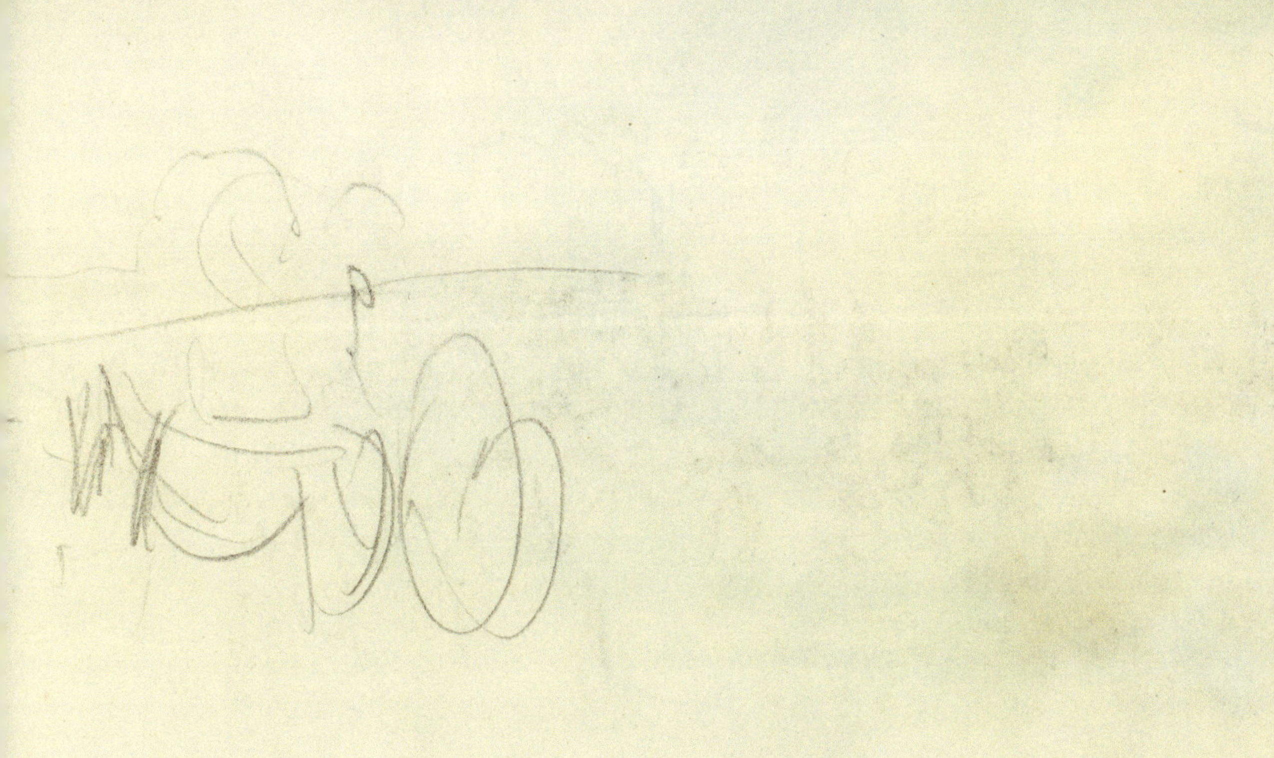

CLVIII - 68

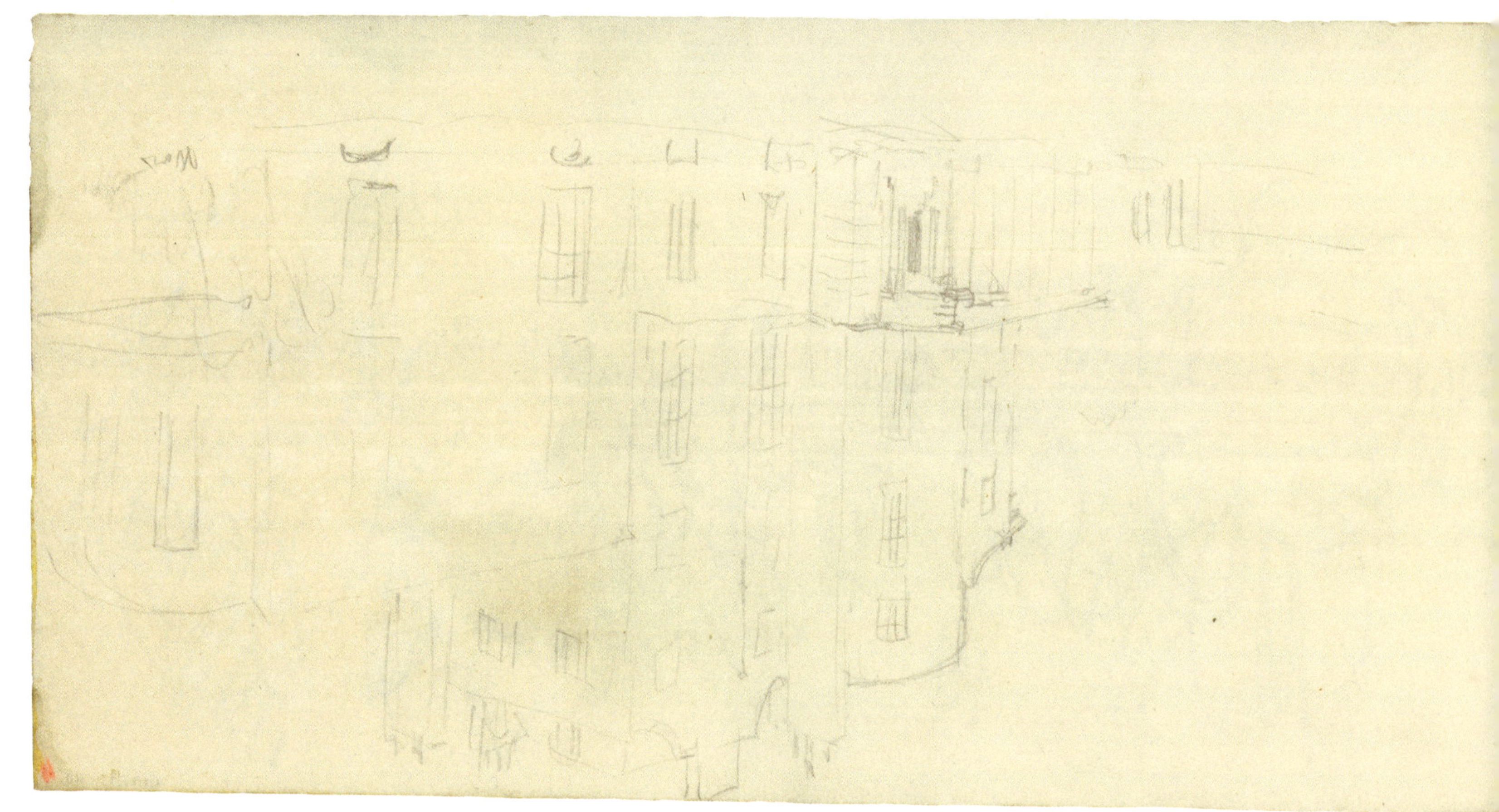

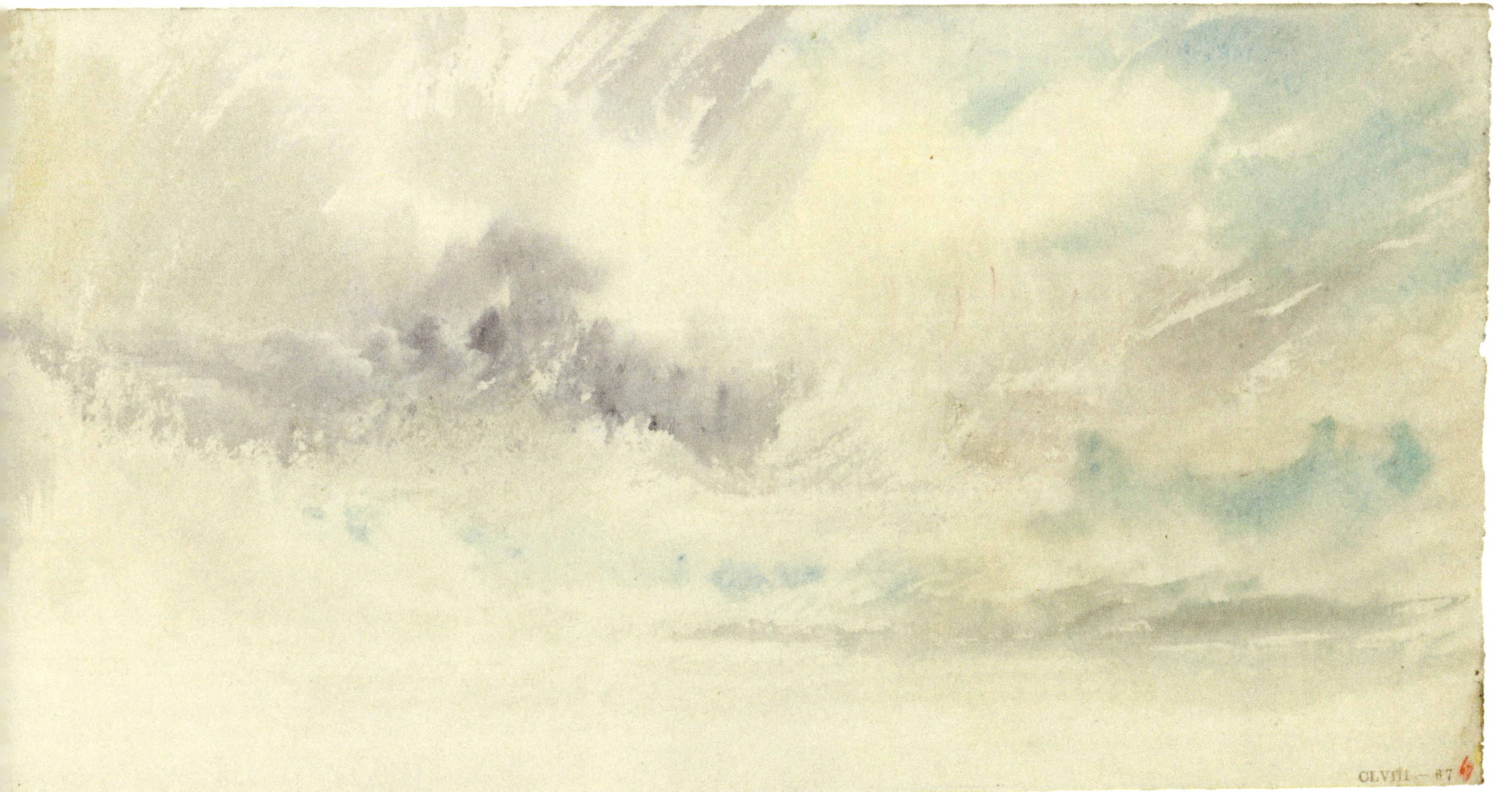

CLVIII – 87

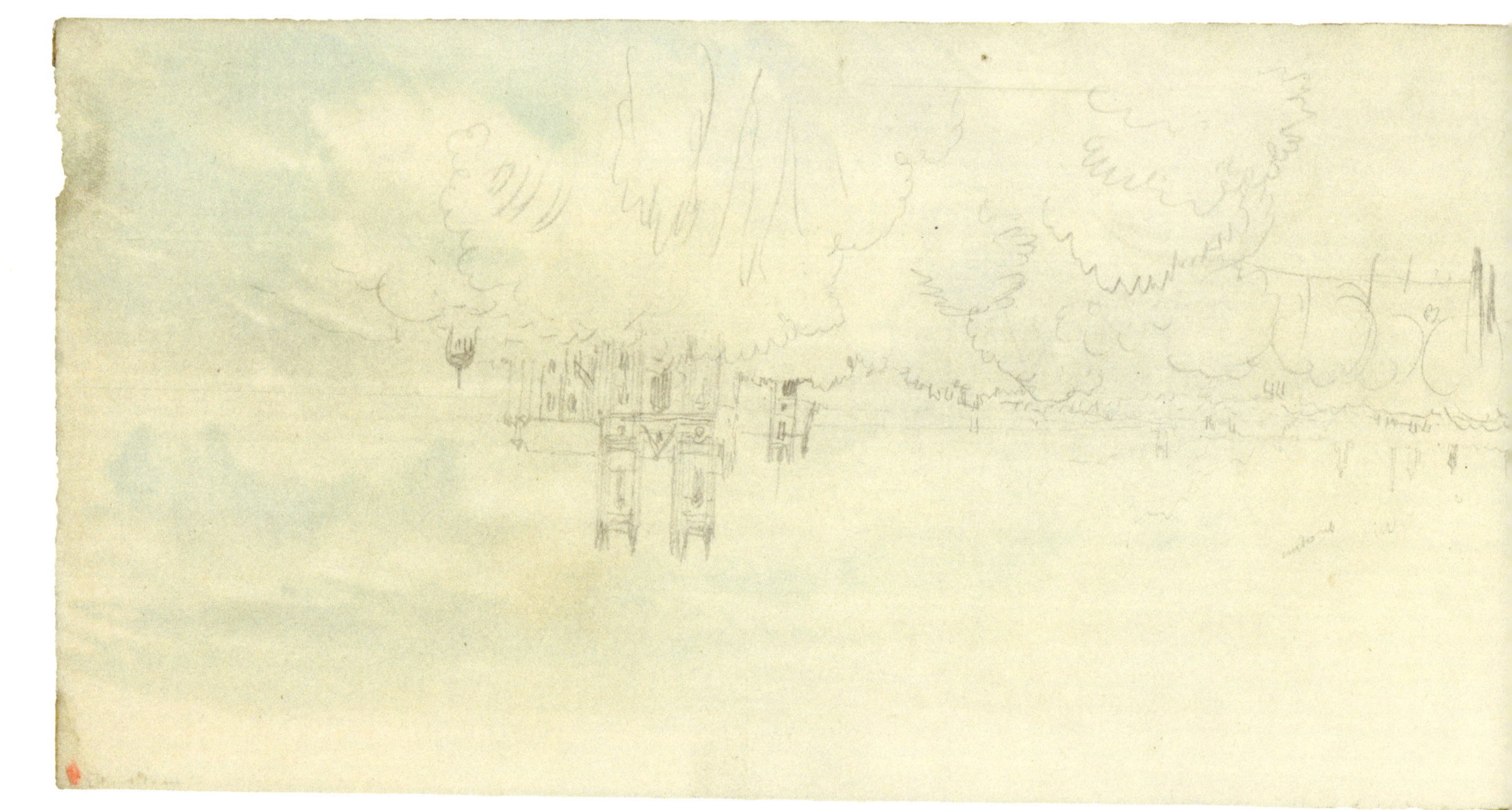

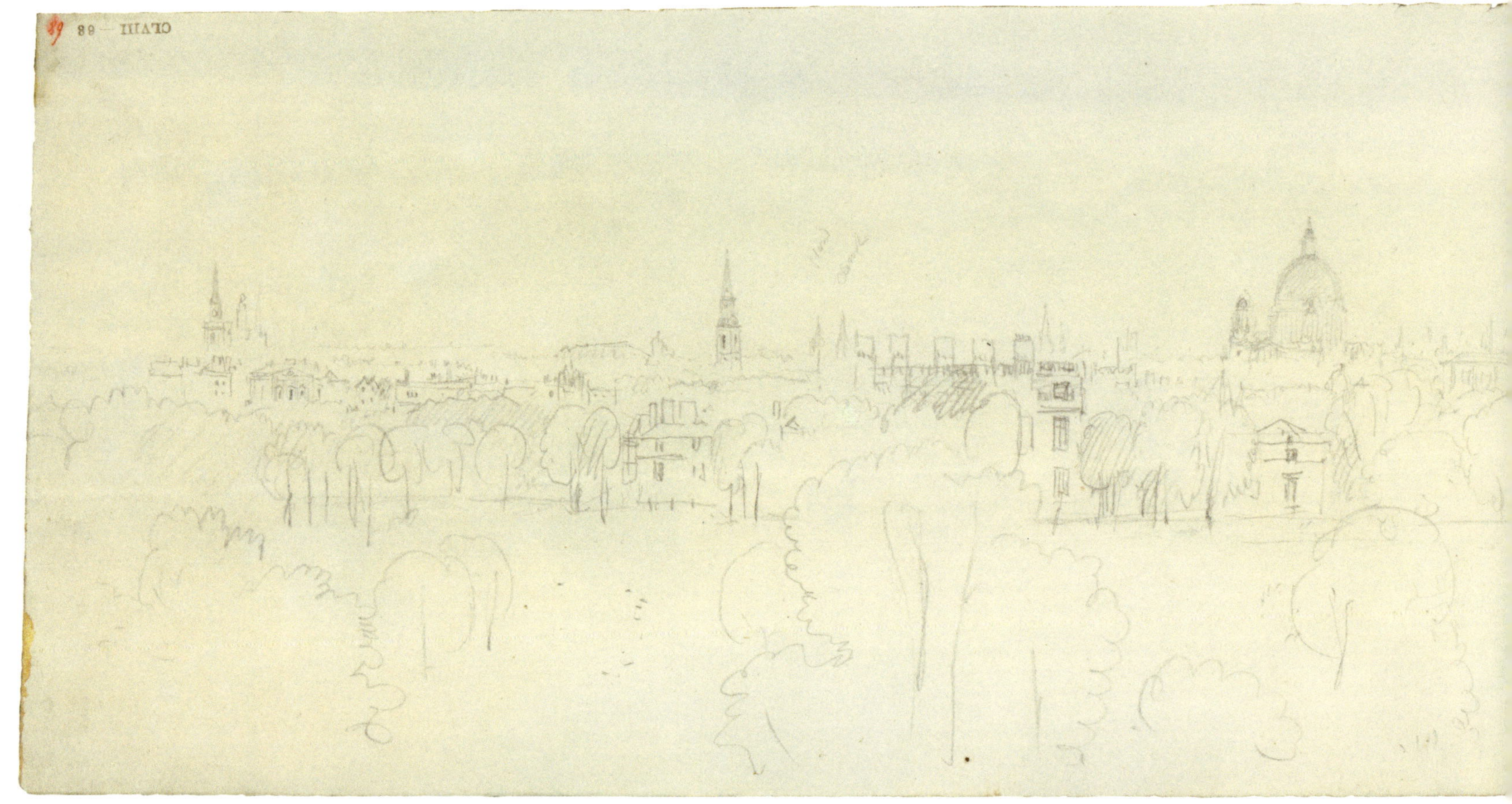

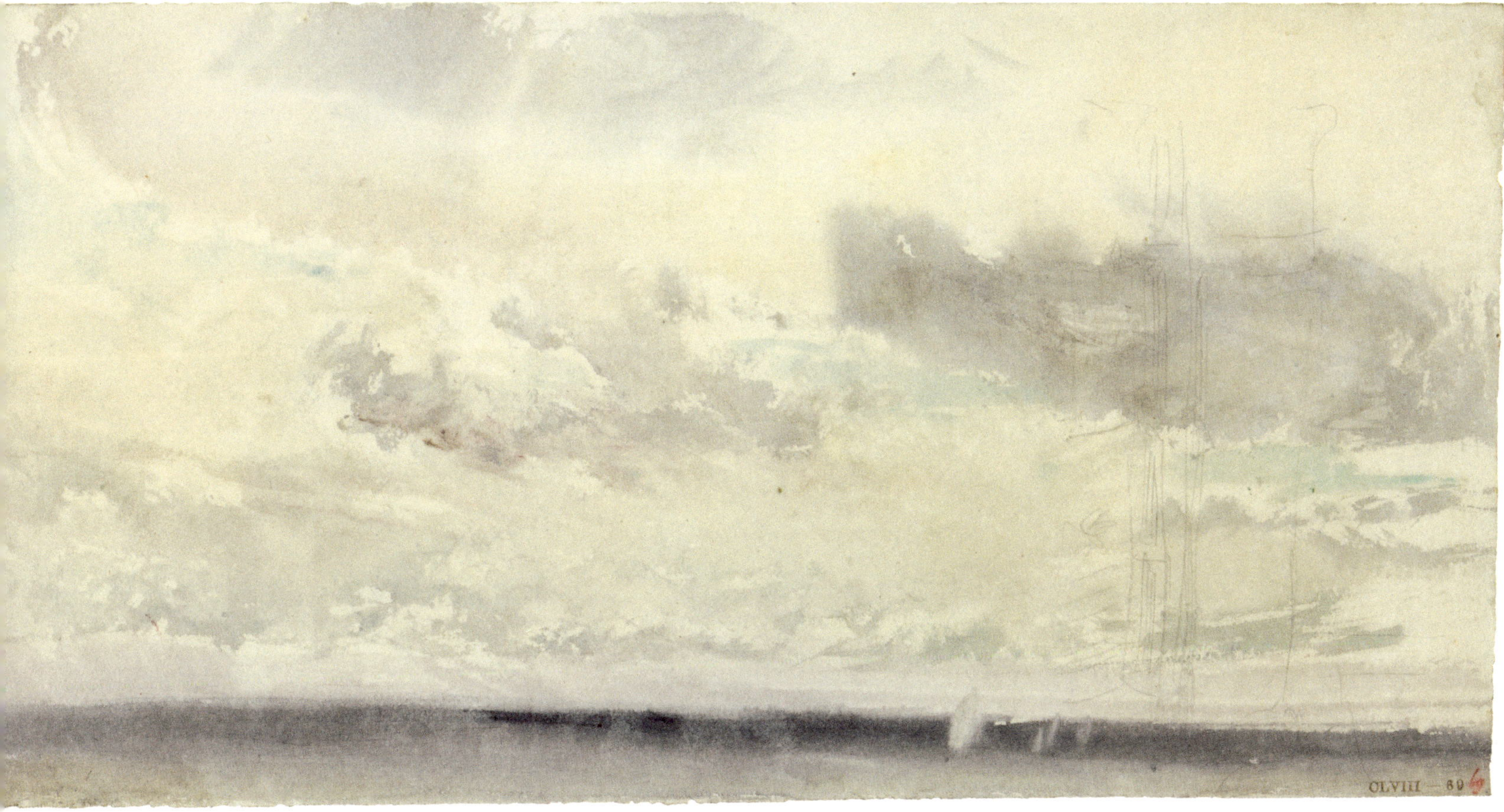
CLVIII — 69

yellochre

Blue shadows Red Crimson Lake

3

12 3

50
3
256